Cheryl Robson

Australian-born, Cheryl worked at the BBC in London for several years then developed and produced new writing for theatre before founding Aurora Metro Books, publishing over 200 writers and winning numerous awards. She has edited several collections of drama from around the world.

As a playwright, she won the Croydon Warehouse International Playwriting Competition, was longlisted for the Bruntwood Prize and has had several stage plays produced.

Her co-translation of *David's Story* by Stig Dalager was shortlisted for the Marsh Award for Children's Literature in Translation and her co-edited book *Silent Women: Pioneers of Cinema* (Supernova) was voted best book on silent film in 2017. As a documentary film director, her film *Rock 'n' Roll Island* won four awards at US film festivals, was nominated at Raindance, London and is to be broadcast on BBC4.

In 2018, she produced *Sight/Unseen,* a conference on Asian Drama at Goldsmiths College, University of London, and Tara Arts in London. In 2019, she worked with IDRF to produce a showcase of Indonesian Plays in London and was a finalist in the ITV National Diversity Awards, for Lifetime Achievement.

First published in the UK in 2019 by Aurora Metro Publications Ltd.
67 Grove Avenue, Twickenham, TW1 4HX
www.aurorametro.com   info@aurorametro.com
Facebook.com/AuroraMetroBooks T: @aurorametro Inst: @aurora_metro

The Silent Song of the Genjer Flowers © Faiza Mardzoeki 2019, English translation © Gratiagusti Chananya Rompas and Mikael Johani 2019

Red Janger © Ibed Surgana Yuga 2019, English translation © Andy Fuller 2019

Cut Out © Riyadhus Shalihin 2019, English translation © Alfian Sa'at 2019

Sin © Adaptation Trisa Triandesa 2019, English translation © John H. McGlynn 2019 from the novel *Not a Virgin* © Nuril Basri 2017

Break In © Agnes Christina 2019

Bedfellows © Hanna Fransisca 2018, English translation © Cobina Gillitt 2019

The Makassar Trilogy © Shinta Febriany 2019, English translation © Alfian Sa'at 2019

Production: Peter Fullagar

Cover photo: © Eva Tobing 2019. Actor Alexander Gebe from Komunitas Berkat Yakin Lampung plays the role of "Lear", on October 7, 2018 at Graha Bakti Budaya in Jakarta, Indonesia.

With thanks to: Marina Tuffier, Harry Read, Ferroccio Viridiani, Maja Florczak

All rights are strictly reserved. For rights enquiries including performing rights please contact the publisher: rights@aurorametro.com

No part of this publication may be reproduced, stored in or introduced into a retrieval system, or transmitted in any form, or by any means (electronic, mechanical, photocopying, recording or otherwise without the prior permission of the publisher. Any person who does any unauthorised act in relation to this publication may be liable to criminal prosecution and civil claims for damages.

This paperback is sold subject to the condition that it shall not, by way of trade or otherwise, be lent, resold, hired out, or otherwise circulated without the publisher's prior consent in any form of binding or cover other than that in which it is published and without a similar condition being imposed on the subsequent purchaser.

Printed in the UK by 4edge Limited.

ISBN: (print) 978-1-912430-39-0

ISBN: (ebook) 978-1-912430-40-6

NEW INDONESIAN PLAYS

ED. CHERYL ROBSON

AURORA METRO BOOKS

some of our other play collections:

Southeast Asian Plays
eds. Cheryl Robson and Aubrey Mellor
ISBN 978-1-906582-86-9   £16.99

British East Asian Plays
eds. C. Robson, A. Rogers, A. Thorpe
ISBN 978-1-912430-08-6 £16.99

A Touch of the Dutch – Plays By Women
Introduced by Mieke Kolk
ISBN 978-0-9515877-7-5   £9.95

New South African Plays
edited and introduced by Charles J. Fourie
ISBN 978-0-9536757-4-6   £12.99

Durban Dialogues, Indian Voice
by Ashwin Singh
ISBN 978-1-906582-42-5   £15.99

Black and Asian Plays Anthology
introduced by Afia Nkrumah
ISBN 978-0-9536757-4-6   £12.99

Six Plays by Black and Asian Women Writers
ed. Kadija George
ISBN 978-0-9515877-2-0   £12.99

www.aurorametro.com

CONTENTS

FOREWORD 7
by Gunawan Maryanto and Muhammad Abe

INTRODUCTION & ABOUT THE PLAYS 10
by Rebecca Kezia

THE SILENT SONG OF THE GENJER FLOWERS 23
by Faiza Mardzoeki
translated by Gratiagusti Chananya Rompas & Mikael Johani

RED JANGER 59
by Ibed Surgana Yuga
translated by Andy Fuller

CUT OUT 83
by Riyadhus Shalihin
translated by Alfian Sa'at

SIN 101
adapted by Trisa Triandesa from the novel
Not a Virgin by Nuril Basri
translated by John H. McGlynn

BREAK IN 123
by Agnes Christina

BEDFELLOWS 145
by Hanna Fransisca
translated by Cobina Gillitt

THE MAKASSAR TRILOGY 171
by Shinta Febriany
translated by Alfian Sa'at

FOREWORD

Gunawan Maryanto and Muhammad Abe

First held in 2010, the Indonesia Dramatic Reading Festival (IDRF) introduces new plays to Indonesian audiences, by offering an annual festival of dramatic readings, open to the public. Over the last nine years, IDRF has featured sixty plays from both Indonesian and international playwrights, presented mostly in Yogyakarta.

The goal of IDRF is to accelerate the development of playwriting within the Indonesian theatre scene. The festival is supported by Teater Garasi and Teater Gardanalla, two Yogyakarta-based theatre companies which mostly write and produce their own new plays. The founders of IDRF, Gunawan Maryanto, Joned Suryatmoko and Lusia Neti Cahyani, are members drawn from those two companies, still actively working as theatre practitioners. IDRF is also aiming to raise awareness of the lack of documenting, archiving or recording of plays in general, as well as encouraging playwrights and theatre workers to document, record and archive their own plays.

Since its beginning, IDRF has actively connected with many international theatre networks. However, it was only in 2018 that IDRF first had the opportunity to present Indonesian plays abroad with an invitation to take part in the Jejak Tabi Festival in Kuala Lumpur, where *Bedfellows* by Hanna Fransisca, included in this collection, was featured.

Following on from the success of this event, IDRF was invited by the Indonesian National Book Committee to organize a showcase of Indonesian plays in London as part of the fringe events during the London Book Fair 2019, where Indonesia was the country of Market Focus.

This provided an exciting opportunity to select and translate several new Indonesian plays into English, which often acts as a carrier language for other countries to read and translate the work. There are few published anthologies of Indonesian drama in English translation, the most important being *The Lontar Anthology of Indonesian Drama* (Lontar Foundation, 2007 – 10), a three volume collection, which ended their selection of plays in 1998. Very few

Indonesian plays from the year 2000 onwards have been translated or published in English. One exception to this, is IDRF co-founder Joned Suryatmoko's play *Piknik*, translated by Barbara Hatley, which was included in Aurora Metro's comprehensive *Southeast Asian Plays* collection, co-edited by Aubrey Mellor and Cheryl Robson (2016). Joned was subsequently invited in 2018 to take part in 'Sight-Unseen', an Asian drama conference at Goldsmiths, University of London and Tara Arts Theatre, where his play *Piknik* was also featured and discussed.

For what would be the first-ever showcase of Indonesian plays in the UK, we began by selecting plays from a nominated pool of fifteen plays that were written between 2000–2018 and ten plays from the period 1950–1999. The nominated plays demonstrated different types of writing and came from a diverse group of writers from different regions in Indonesia. Gunawan Maryanto and Muhammad Abe, who have both been part of the IDRF team since its inception, made the difficult final selection of just six plays. The chosen plays covered a range of social and political issues such as problems of urban development, new interpretations of historical events, ongoing racial and ethnic conflict, gender equality and sexual orientation.

The showcase, called appropriately 'First Date', was held at Ovalhouse Theatre in south London from May 7-9 2019, in association with Aurora Metro Books. Of the six Indonesian plays featured, four of them were written in the last decade, and translated especially for the event, while two others were classic Indonesian plays (*Moths* by Arifin C Noer, translated by Harry Aveling, and *Things Growing on the Table* by Afrizal Malna, translated by Michael Bodden). The plays were read by London-based actors, many of whom were of East Asian descent, and it was a great experience not only to witness Indonesian plays being performed abroad by talented actors but also to see them being well-received by the audience. There was also a good post-show discussion with the curators which gave the audience a chance to engage and ask questions about the work. Following the success of 'First Date', Muhammad Abe began to work closely with Cheryl Robson at Aurora Metro to develop and publish this anthology, so that Indonesian drama could be promoted more widely to international readers.

FOREWORD

This anthology consists of four of the modern plays which were featured in the showcase in London, as well as three other contemporary plays that were nominated but did not have the chance to be featured in 'First Date'. We hope that reading this anthology will give readers a greater understanding of Indonesia and its theatre scene, and an appreciation of the plays collected herein.

For this publication we would like to thank editor, Cheryl Robson, and Aurora Metro Books, Dewi Noviami, John McGlynn, Nataresmi and the National Book Committee for their support of both the showcase and publication. We are grateful too for the great work of the translators, namely Alfian Sa'at, Andy Fuller, Cobina Gillitt, John H. McGlynn, Gratiagusti Chananya Rompas, Mikael Johani and editing by Kumiko Mendl and Max Lane. We would like to say thank you to the directors Rosamunde Hutt, Kumiko Mendl and Jen Tan and to the many actors who were involved in the 'First Date' showcase in London. Last but not least, we are grateful to the seven fine playwrights in this publication. We hope that this will be the launchpad for the publication of a new series of Indonesian plays.

Enjoy the plays and see you around!

Gunawan Maryanto

Born in 1976 in Yogyakarta, he is an actor, director, poet and playwright. A member of Teater Garasi, one of the leading contemporary theatre companies in Indonesia. Gunawan is one of the curators of the Asia Playwrights Meeting. He frequently publishes his fiction and poetry in Indonesian daily newspapers. He is one of the founders of the Indonesian Dramatic Reading Festival.

Muhammad Abe

Muhammad was born in 1985, in Pati. He is an actor, writer and researcher. After finishing his Masters degree in Theatre Studies at Gadjah Mada University, Yogyakarta, Muhammad has been working as a translator, researcher and facilitator for theatre, dance and visual arts events. Muhammad is one of the curators of the Asia Playwrights Meeting and recently curated the first showcase of Indonesian Plays in London.

IDRF is an independent Indonesian script reading festival and is designed to develop organically according to the needs of Indonesian playwrights.

INTRODUCTION

Rebecca Kezia

The practice of playwriting in Indonesia cannot be separated from the development of its theatre scene. They grow together, intertwined, as mediums for social reflection, as portraits of a certain era, or as a series of ideas and concepts emerging from time to time. However, it is not enough for us to look at their development chronologically. Many elements influence and encourage the growth and changes in theatre and playwriting traditions, including socio-political conditions that we experience — from the colonial days to today's post-Reformasi era — as manifested in the institutionalization of works, in language censorship, or even in the issue of primordial identities.

The practice of theatre in Indonesia reaches far back to an undocumented past, when it served as part of ceremonies or rituals. Once detached from its ceremonial aspect, the stage element of a performance gradually became a spectacle to be performed by and for the community it belonged to. This process allows us to now see the uniqueness of the different kinds of folk theatre. Furthermore, because they are exclusive by character — in either language or storyline — folk theatre can only thrive within the context of its home community.

Modern Indonesian theatre was born within a pluralistic social space. The first recorded form of what would become modern theatre in Indonesia is *opera melayu*, most notably Komedie Stamboel, a troupe formed in Surabaya by Auguste Mahieu. The troupe performed works inspired by the classic Arabic tales *A Thousand and One Nights*, presented in a proscenium format — with an invisible 'fourth wall' being raised between the audience and the stories being staged. With its fluid format, more groups were inspired to develop those stories as drama or *toneel*.

Later, the European education system, as introduced by the Dutch in the colonies, influenced how stories were told and how ideas were conveyed. The colonial government also created an atmosphere that exposed the colonies to other cultures, especially by opening up urban marketspaces. Access to new knowledge and new contexts helped the *pribumi* (indigenous people) to develop their own ideas and concepts. Western literature inspired the creation of plays such as *Lelakon Raden Bei Surio Retno* (*Raden Bei Surio's Retreat*) by F. Wiggers in 1901 or *Bebasari* (*Sweet Liberty*) by Rustam Effendi in 1926. Scholars and intellectuals made use of this medium to convey their ideas, especially those connected to rising nationalism against the backdrop of colonialism.

When the Japanese replaced the Dutch in Indonesia, theatre plays became a well-utilized means of spreading their Greater East Asia propaganda. Much like the formation of Balai Pustaka that forced literary works to be written and published in a specific language — namely *Melayu* language — Japanese propaganda became a censorial force that controlled how theatre plays were written. Literary works, especially drama, were thick with militaristic Greater East Asia propaganda. Meanwhile, Usmar Ismail, one of the great figures in Indonesian theatre and film, managed to find a way to use this limitation to reflect on humanity without overtly criticizing Japanese policies, such as can be seen in *Citra* (1943).

Indonesia declared its independence following Japan's defeat in World War II, which also meant a shift in arts dynamics across the nation. Theatre practitoners searched for their identities and spoke of revolution through realist dramas that highlighted ideological conflicts, as exemplified by *Bunga Rumah Makan* (*The Welcome Meal*) by Utuy Tatang Sontani in 1948. While they were contending with tense identity politics, Absurdist plays such as those by Ionesco entered the country and influenced Indonesian playwrights to consider/explore existentialism. Meanwhile, the Indonesian Communist Party, through its cultural institution Lembaga Kebudayaan Rakyat (Lekra), believed that art must aim to be something that could better people's lives, not just as a process towards artistic achievement. To further its propaganda, the Communist Party chose to employ folk theatre, which was more popular amongst the proletariat. However, this also led to a decrease in the number of new plays and theatre works being produced.

Dramatic plays once again became a popular performance medium when the New Order regime — in the spirit of development, progress and stability — opened up spaces for discourse as widely as possible.

In its attempt to achieve stability, the government aimed to build Jakarta into a centre with a solid footing internationally. This was realized under the governorship of Ali Sadikin, who established Taman Ismail Marzuki (TIM) to provide some element of protection for artists working under the authoritarian New Order Regime that heavily regulated cultural output and prohibited free speech. It was to act as an extension of the government to both control and nurture art and artistic practices as a new industry. The government appointed a number of artists to manage TIM, collectively known as Akademi Jakarta, which in turn routinely appointed other artists to manage arts programs through Dewan Kesenian Jakarta (Jakarta Arts Council). Through this institution, theatre work and playwriting enjoyed a second golden age, after a previous high in the 1950s (during the Old Order). Programs were created in abundance, and in an indirect way they helped to determine the artists' workflow. Theatre festivals and competitions helped to create a sustainable flow of both funding and audiences to nurture a good arts ecosystem, encouraging both theatre and playwriting.

A 'new wind' blowing through the first act of the New Order era also helped to build other art centres outside of Jakarta, such as in Yogyakarta, Bandung and Padangpanjang. Research centres and art schools were successively established in those places. Overseas student exchanges and residency programs were widely offered as part of cultural promotion and development. Jakob Sumardjo, who has chronicled the development of modern Indonesian theatre, noted that in the 1970s, up to 47 original plays were produced. His research also revealed that they were predominantly focused on social issues, metaphysics and psychology.

In those days, playwriting was mostly developed by theatre directors or theatre practitioners. One of the most influential figures was W. S. Rendra, who founded Bengkel Teater, which performed original plays that he had either written or translated from Western works. This group nurtured the next generation of playwrights and theatre directors such as Arifin C Noer, Putu Wijaya and Nano Riantiarno. Rendra received an art scholarship grant to study in the United States. When he returned, he brought with him a style that influenced directors to explore textless or non-verbal performances, dubbed *teater minikata* (theatre with an economy of words).

In addition to external influences that were introduced to Indonesia through institutional programs and cooperation/collaborations — such as explorations of textless performances, or of ideologies that question single narratives by single groups, or post-modernist explorations — the politicization of art became another reason why artists sought new articulations for their concepts. The New Order regime's centralized policies forced playwrights and artists to position themselves as part of the community. During the second part of the New Order, there was almost no gap left between the plays being written by playwrights and the lives they led or the community where they/their group belonged. Here, we could draw a line back to our earlier discussion regarding the origins of folk theatre. The language being employed became lighter and more conversational. Underdog characters began to emerge as heroes criticizing a totalitarian government. Poverty was not just a topic of discussion but also the main point of conflict in a play. See, for example, works by playwrights such as Arifin, Riantiarno, Putu and Rendra himself.

Attempts to deformalize language as a form of protest against the government's autocratic control over an ideological subject could also be found in a style of playwriting that was neither linear, nor absurd, nor did it employ conventional logic. Look, for instance, at plays by Afrizal Malna or those undocumented Payung Hitam performances (led by Rachman Sabur) emerging in the third act of the New Order. These plays utilized data as story or character, not just as subjects driving a plot but as extraordinary serendipities disrupting politically fabricated spaces. One such example is *Pertumbuhan di Meja Makan* (*Things Growing on the Dining Table*) by Afrizal Malna, first staged in 1991, that employs a postmodern strategy by piecing together bits of text from different sources. Another example is Putu Wijaya's play *Aduh* (*Ought*), published in 1973. Wijaya attempted to 'terrorize' his audiences so that they would reconsider their conventional understanding of the world. Thus, we do not find words that fit a rational understanding, nor do we come across characters who communicate normally to convey an idea.

Interestingly, the government reacted much more swiftly towards alternative protests that were conveyed in a lighter, more comical and entertaining manner, such as what was done by Riantiarno through Teater Koma. Perhaps because on these occasions, politics were being laughed at, policies were being made fun of, and heroic aspects of the New Order regime — like its vision and mission — were transformed into songs and hijinks on Teater Koma's stages, such as in *Opera Kecoa* (*Cockroach Opera*) in 1983 and *Opera Ikan Asin* (*A Salted Fish Opera*, adapted from Bertolt Brecht's play *The Threepenny Opera*) in 1985. Teater Gandrik in Yogyakarta also went a similar route, offering hybrid Javanese folk theatre, generously peppered with regional languages, perhaps as a way to evade censorship or even to play with the logic of censorship itself.

Ideological clashes between artistic expression — especially by those involved in theatre and literature — and government power towards the end of the New Order, created a number of characteristics that we can still see, even today, in the practice of theatre and playwriting.

First, playwriting as a means of theatre work. Here, the existence of a play is highly dependent upon the level of productivity of a given theatre group. In this case, the group's theatre director or member(s) wrote plays, usually due to the submission schedules of theatre competitions or festivals that required original plays. For instance, the annual Festival Teater Jakarta held at TIM has separate categories evaluating and marketing original plays. Unfortunately, play creation was not always well-supported by play documentation, perhaps because playscripts are mainly seen as a mere instrument, as a means to a production, or simply due to the lack of resources to conduct proper documentation. To date, only original plays submitted to Festival Teater Jakarta from 2006 – 2013 have been located, in which recurring themes were found, such as poverty and existentialism, as well as plays focusing on experimental staging.

One theatre group still actively performing and creating new plays is Teater Koma, founded by N. Riantarno in 1977. They have presented more than 100 plays to date, and are looking to do many more. Unfortunately, there are a number of groups that emerged prior to the Reformasi era that have had to step back for many reasons, such as the death of their founders or theatre directors e.g. Rendra's Bengkel Teater and Teguh Karya's Teater Populer. Meanwhile, we also note the many theatre groups on the festival or university campus circuit that perform adaptations from, or translations of, foreign works.

Next, since restrictions on free speech were lifted at the end of the New Order in 1998, we see stage work that seeks its form from the embodiment of text or from prior-present-future events. Theatre work of this kind often becomes a laboratory that is less preoccupied with the final product, choosing instead to concentrate on how issues can be discussed or examined through data. Here, theatre groups translate data into stories, and each stage becomes an incubatory process aiming to come up with new possibilities. Teater Garasi, Lab Teater Ciputat and Kala Teater are examples of groups representing this idea. In Teater Garasi's works, for instance, texts or plays are often not required to start a performance; rather plays can be developed over several performances, causing changes in narratives and visuals from one stage to the next.

Research-based theatre work is usually supported by collaborations that interrogate regional (Asian) or historical socio-political identities. Usually, writers come from different disciplines — anthropology, science, even philosophy. Groups are formed through exchange programs that provide opportunities and access for artists to explore diverse artistic forms, but also through a clear effort to decentralize control, especially over how ideas are conveyed. There is a conscious effort to interrogate prevailing single historical narratives. In this process of decentralization and reform, art — especially theatre and its texts — once again acts as a fluid and informal means of communication.

Third, playwriting as textual awareness that is present in forms other than those purely for performance. These plays do not need to be written by people directly connected to theatre groups, and nor do they need a performance for completion. Rather, they are written based on an understanding that plays are unique modes of literary expression. Instead, playwrights often use dramatic forms as a way to enter into a dialogue with abstract ideas or concepts. This genre of writing grows steadily thanks to the many platforms supporting playwrights such as IDRF (Indonesia Dramatic Reading Festival),

Bengkel Penulisan Naskah (Playwriting Workshop), Asosiasi Penulis Naskah Drama Indonesia (The Indonesian Dramatic Writers Association), as well as through the publication of play anthologies by independent or institutional publishers.

Although their writing styles might derive inspiration from pre-existing forms, they usually offer new viewpoints. See for instance, efforts to rewrite 'horror and women' through the publication of *Antologi Naskah Drama Rawayan 2019, Kisah Nyai Dasima (The Story of Nyai Dasima)* — various sources — and *Si Manis Jembatan Ancol (The Sweet Ancol Bridge)*. Efforts to create new embodiments of old existing tales often lead to discussion about the proximity of such works to our daily lives and the importance of actualizing existing discourses. We find a similar vein in Ibed Surgana Yuga's *Janger Merah (Red Janger)*, written as an interrogation of history through realist approaches. Drama is chosen as a communication strategy that can bring discourses closer to the readers. The same intent could be felt in Hanna Fransisca's *Teman Tidur (Bedfellows)*.

This reworking of well-known stories can also be seen as a strategy to attract support for their production. By creating new works in this way, we find opportunities for collaborations that are not limited to particular theatre groups or theatre practitioners. The above three forms are not intended to be closed categories. Rather they should only serve as a starting point to help us further map the relationships and developments within theatre work and playwriting. They don't always walk hand-in-hand, but they need each other. As long as human issues or problems exist, dramatic plays will continue as an avenue of communication. They can serve as an important stage in artistic development, which is oftentimes required for artist self-actualization and motivation to contribute to the world.

Dramatic forms will always change, fitting themselves to the spaces and resources available at a given time, especially in today's digital era with its quick flow of information. This has directly affected the artistic development and discourse in the arts, including theatre and drama. Many text and stage works are trying to explore the possibility of new artistic forms in the available technological approaches, for example a new multimedia form of theatre which combines projected images and videos with live performance enabling us to question the complex ways we are represented in the media, such as in Naomi Srikandi's *Medea Media*. The pages of social media and the interactions recorded in them become a new reality that changes the social view of the author in composing the text of the plays. It becomes a showcase of discourse, and found its dramatic form as written in Shohifur Ridho'I's play *Tiga Lapis Kesedihan* (*Three Layers of Sadness*).

New technology has opened up opportunities and experimental space that was previously unimaginable, breaking the boundary between reality and the stage with AR and VR technology to bring the audience in to be part of the event. Social media spaces could also be used as new meeting rooms for the audience and the artists. The distance between the arts and the audience is increasingly blurred in technological advancements. However, this also means a change in our reading of theatrical events. It might not only shift the way we are used to confronting conflict and issues, experiment and aesthetic, but also the way we include the public as part of the event itself. The elimination of certain values and the shifting of ethics will be another factor in shaping the new landscape of plays and theatre. In Indonesia, many theatre works have also used the support of a dramaturg and spectator dramaturg to extend the original concept.

This is a very exciting time for us to embrace the possibilities ahead offering us new perspectives on narrating our story. Moreover, theatre, through its dramatic and text documentation, offers us a communal space for reflection and social discourse that can help us to once again look at ourselves and the march of time in a critical way.

Rebecca Kezia

Rebecca graduated from the University of Indonesia in Indonesia Studies Major with a focus on Modern Literature in 2014, with her thesis on Indonesian Plays of Jakarta Theatre Festival 2006-2013.

She is actively involved in several projects such as working as Guest Curator for the Indonesia Dramatic Reading Festival and recently contributed in Jakarta Theatre Platform's exhibition of Latest Indonesian Plays entitled "Ruang Riuh".

Currently working in Komunitas Salihara as Education and Discourse Program Coordinator. She is also active as a performer and playwright.

ABOUT THE PLAYS

This collection aims to give the reader a taste of the variety of modern plays being written and performed in Indonesia since the year 2000. The aim was to find plays which give insight into Indonesian communities as well as offering interesting playtexts to perform. It includes three innovative dramatic works which play with narrative, form and/or stage conventions, namely *The Makassar Trilogy*, *Cut Out* and *Break In*, as well as more naturalistic dramas such as *Red Janger, The Silent Song of the Genjer Flowers* and *Bedfellows*, which have been performed internationally.

Sin, a stage adaptation of a novel, offers insight into the LGBTQ community in Indonesia, demonstrating how the conflict between traditional religious teaching and Western permissiveness is played out among the younger generation.

Red Janger finds comedy in the grisly tale of a former massacre, in which villager was forced to turn on villager. The shadow left by the Suharto years is still very much in evidence.

The Makassar Trilogy incorporates research data, verbatim interviews and poetry within a single play to try and distil the experiences of those displaced by a beach reclamation project into theatrical form.

THE SILENT SONG OF THE GENJER FLOWERS
by Faiza Mardzoeki, translated by Gratiagusti Chananya Rompas & Mikael Johani

Faiza Mardzoeki is an established playwright with many productions both at home and abroad. In this all-female play, a group of five women friends aged between 70 and 83 come together after a long time. One of them wants to tell the truth about a long-held family secret to her granddaughter, Ming, but is afraid of her reaction. The women revisit their memories of happier times in their youth, before they were all imprisoned in 1965 under the Suharto regime's crackdown on communism. Not only did they endure lengthy prison terms when they suffered sexual violence, they have also had to face social stigma since their release. Ming has lived behind a veil of mystery about her grandmother's life, and during the play she must bear witness to the women's experiences and come to terms with their suffering. The play raises awareness of an important period in Indonesian history, little known by the current generation.

RED JANGER
by Ibed Surgana Yuga, translated by Andy Fuller

Bali is most known for its wonderful beaches and tourist resorts, but playwright Ibed Surgana Yuga, who was born and raised in Bali, is always challenging this beautiful image that is promoted for the sake of tourism. In *Red Janger*, Ibed uses "Janger", which is a popular folk dance performed across Bali for the locals and tourists, to recall the origins of the folk dance. This darkly humorous play, featuring two headless ghosts who walk the streets in limbo and a local Balinese family, shows a different understanding of politics between two generations of the same family, and the issues that arise when the troubled past of Bali is revisited due to the uncovering of a mass grave that was hidden near a schoolyard.

CUT OUT
by Riyadhus Shalihin, translated by Alfian Sa'at

An experimental play by a young Indonesian playwright that was created by digging through the visual archives of Indonesian history. Riyadhus, who is studying theatre and visual arts, has collected numerous images from Indonesian history and put them together with a free-ranging narrative text. *Cut Out*, translated by Singaporean Alfian Sa'at, offers us a glimpse of Indonesian history in a multi-media form. Riyadhus has chosen to combine the big historical narratives (the nation, the important person in history, the main event) together with the smaller tales and events from history (the *kampong*, the common, the side event). This mash-up of times, people and places provides a new way of understanding the connections and similarities between the past and present as an ongoing continuum. *Cut Out* is the second play in a trilogy by Riyadhus.

SIN
adapted by Trisa Triandesa from the novel *Not a Virgin* by Nuril Basri, translated by John H. McGlynn

In a country with a Muslim majority population, *Sin* is an unusual play depicting the lives of a small minority who are rarely portrayed in the media. Following the novel *Not a Virgin* by Nuril Basri, this stage adaptation is centred on a group of *santri* (young students in a *pesantren* or Muslim boarding school) who frequently visit nightclubs in their spare time. Bored with the daily routine in their religious school, they go in search of fun in the local town. They learn ways of getting money outside of the boarding school through sex work and drag queen contests. Actor and playwright Trisa Triandesa shows how they become increasingly at odds with the moral guardians of the town, with devastating consequences.

BREAK IN
by Agnes Christina

An absurd drama between a daughter, her mother and a gecko, which transports us into the fantasy world of a young woman, frightened to go outside. The play is set in a family home, where a lonely daughter starts to talk with a gecko, who can go into her mother's room and watch what goes on. As her isolation increases, she also forms relationships with the door to her room, the girl in the mirror, and later in a surreal, hallucinatory scene, she talks to a kettle, developing a friendship with them all. However, *Break In* deals with more than loneliness, as it portrays a daughter who is unable to connect with her mother and shows how identity and personal space relate to family beliefs and religion. Playwright and director Agnes Christina, who lived for many years in Singapore, chose to write her play in English and then later wrote a version in Indonesian.

BEDFELLOWS
by Hanna Fransisca, translated by Cobina Gillitt

Hanna Fransisca is one of the few Chinese-Indonesian women playwrights in Indonesia, who is also recognised as a poet and fiction writer. *Bedfellows* tells the story of a group of Chinese-Indonesian people living in West Kalimantan at a time of transition during a rise in inter-ethnic conflict between the Chinese-Indonesian and Muslim communities. The play is set in a popular coffee shop, owned by a Chinese-Indonesian woman, that has become the meeting point for traffickers selling girls to Taiwanese businessmen as wives. When the play opens, it becomes apparent that a Naga statue in town, revered by the local Chinese-Indonesian community, has become a flashpoint of contention, threatening to set long-time friends against each other. The play offers a hard-hitting portrait of a multicultural city that is on the cusp of change.

THE MAKASSAR TRILOGY
by Shinta Febriany, translated by Alfian Sa'at

The Makassar Trilogy consists of three short plays by Shinta Febriany and her collaborators, as part of the City Theatre Project developed by Shinta and Kala Teater in Makassar, South Sulawesi, Indonesia. The play is based on the research undertaken by Shinta, Kala Teater, and her collaborators (a poet, a writer and a filmmaker based in Makassar) into the impact of recent urban development on its citizens. They interpreted the data that was collected by Kala Teater and translated it into a performance text.

The first play in the trilogy, titled *Don't Die Before He Arrives*, tells the story of the rising number of suicides by Makassar's citizens between 2016-2017. The second play, titled *The Madness of the Mad* explores the rising number of people with mental illness and those who are homeless in Makassar city. The third play, titled *Give Me the Old Beach*, tells the sorry story of the beach reclamation to create exclusive housing that destroyed the old beach. The trilogy includes verbatim interviews with local residents, a re-enactment of a scene that the actors observe, quotes from the newspaper and television news, and poetic responses to the data. In performance, each play is presented in a different space which the audience walk through.

Playwright's note: This play was written based on interviews with 65 women survivors as well as interviewing their families and children to see how the past has affected the next generation. In addition to interviews, I researched secondary source material and read various historical archives.

My play, *The Silent Song of the Genjer Flowers,* reveals the truth about women activists in Gerwani – the Indonesian Women's Movement – who were made political prisoners and suffered sexual violence during the political upheaval in Indonesia between 1965–68 and onwards. During that time, hundreds of thousands of members of the Communist Party of Indonesia (PKI), or those considered close to the PKI, were murdered and tens of thousands also imprisoned. Out of this upheaval came the military backed New Order regime, under General Suharto.

Misinformation about the savagery of Gerwani women was spread by the military and mainstream media to justify massacres that occurred in various regions. This propaganda claimed, falsely, that communist women had danced naked in front of detained generals, slit their genitals and otherwise tortured them before they were shot dead. Official autopsies, kept secret for decades, showed that there was no torture. The story was a total slander.

Saskia Wieringa argued in *Sexual Politics in Indonesia* that the New Order regime legitimized itself through the demonization of female sexuality, deliberately portraying women activists as monsters to evoke fear of communism among youth and religious groups. It led to the removal of women from the political realm and repositioned women as obedient to, and dependent on, men.

In fact, Gerwani was a women's organization that fought for women's rights in economic, social, cultural and educational areas. The government propaganda has erased the important role of Gerwani in the history of the women's movement in Indonesia from the national memory and stigmatized those who were involved in the movement.

The Silent Song of the Genjer Flowers offers a counter-discourse to the official history of the New Order by presenting the perspectives of former female political prisoners and shows how they have struggled after their release, in a society that continues to reject them.

THE SILENT SONG OF THE GENJER FLOWERS

Faiza Mardzoeki

translated by Gratiagusti Chananya Rompas and Mikael Johani
Editor: Max Lane

This play is dedicated to the women political prisoners from 1965 and victims of sexual violence in Indonesia and everywhere.

Characters
MINGHAYATI DAYANINA (MING)
— 25 years old, the granddaughter of Nini
GRANDMOTHER SUHARTINI (NINI) — 85 years old
SULAHANA — 83 years old
MAKMIN — 76 years old
TARWIH — 80 years old
SUMILAH — 73 years old

Stage Setting
The stage is divided into three sections. To the left is Grandma Nini's bedroom with a simple single bed. The room has one door. In a corner, but not far from the centre of the area is a small wardrobe. In the central area of the stage is a simple sofa. On the right side of the stage is a circular dining table with six chairs. There is a brown batik table cloth.

Time: 2014

SCENE 1

Grandma Nini is lying on the bed, embracing a worn cloth doll. Ming is massaging her grandmother Nini's feet.

Ming stands up, takes a few steps and turns to look back at her grandmother. Then walks slowly to the sofa and sits down. She begins to speak.

MING I am not sure how I should start this story. There are too many things I find hard to understand. But, I must tell you. It is too heavy a burden to carry by myself.

NINI *(still lies on her bed. Speaks slowly, rasping. She calls weakly a name)* Rachma... Rachma...

MING *(turns to look at Nini on bed)* The woman lying there is my grandmother. I call her Grandma Nini.

Nini slowly sits up. Her body is bent. Her hair is white and is a mess.

MING *(startled, she takes Nini's hand)* You're awake, Grandma?

NINI What time is it?

MING *(caressing Nini's forehead)* Grandma has a fever. You still have a temperature. Just lie down and rest, yes?

NINI I have a meeting this afternoon. You know that. I can't be late. It is an important meeting.

MING What meeting, Grandma? There is no meeting. You must rest.

NINI I told you, there is a meeting on at the Kramat office. Where is that ivory, yellow kebaya of mine?

Nini brushes Ming away. Nini gets her strength back, even though bent and a little unsteady. She opens her wardrobe looking for clothes.

NINI Where is that ivory, yellow kebaya of mine, Ming? Ah... here it is, I found it. *(She takes her kebaya. She stares at her kebaya. Then she sits on the edge of the bed. She caresses the kebaya folded in her lap. Ming observes her.)* Ming, what is the date today?

MING Seventh August. Why, Grandma? *(surprised)*

NINI Oh... Not the 20th of June?
MING No.
NINI But we have guests today, yes?
MING Your guests are coming tomorrow, Gran. You should get some more sleep, okay?

Nini is quiet. She looks around unfocused.

NINI Forgive your Grandma, Ming.

Nini takes the doll and embraces it, sitting on the bed. Ming lets out a long sigh. She gazes at Nini on the bed.

NINI *(sad)* Rachma, where are you! Why do you never come home?

Ming stands not far from Nini.

MING Rachma was my mother. On her 20th birthday, in 1986, she married. She was happy. A baby was born out of that happy marriage. That baby was me. Yet their happiness did not last long. *(exits stage)*

SCENE 2

Nini is still sitting on the bed and is still rocking the doll, then she speaks again.

NINI I could only enjoy and see your crying and laughter for a short while, Rachma. I had only breastfed you for three months when you were taken away from me. A distant relative agreed to take you. But she made me promise never to tell you who your real mother was. Ties with the past had to be severed, so you could grow up as a normal child. That was what she said. Oh, my child, my Rachma. I had no choice but to give you up. I did not want you to grow up in prison. *(She stands. She sings a lullaby. She rocks the doll, embraces it and then puts it to sleep on the bed.)* My life was taken away from me. I never imagined that my child would be born behind prison walls. I was moved from prison to prison until finally I was sent to the camp at Plantungan. After fourteen years, I was released. In 1979 to be precise. But I was not really free; there were many conditions to my release. It was the hope of seeing my child that sustained me. Years went by and that hope started to fade. Perhaps Rachma's adopted mother had indeed severed all ties with me, her own mother. Then in 1992, fifteen years after I was released from prison, and exactly on Rachma's birthday... that day my heart was racing, though I didn't know why. I had a feeling something was going to happen. *(She stands. She restlessly looks around as if expecting somebody.)* An elderly woman came to my house. It was that distant relative who had taken my baby from the prison. She had a little girl with her. I was struck silent. *(Pause)* I looked at them closely, was that my Rachmanina? No. Impossible, Rachma was a grown woman by now. I became increasingly anxious. I invited the woman to sit down. Then she explained about the five-year-old girl. Her name was Ming or Minghayati Dayanina. *(Pause)* She told me that Ming was my granddaughter. Oh, I had a granddaughter. I was so happy *(a happy little laugh)*. But it was for only a moment. It was swept away by other news that she passed on to me. *(Pause. Takes a deep breath, sighs.)* Rachmanina had died five years earlier – from post-natal depression and from the distress at being abandoned by her husband. In a trembling voice, she told me how Rachma's husband had abandoned her after he found out that she was born in prison from the womb of a woman who was a political prisoner. *(She sits down on the bed again holding in her sadness.)* Suddenly I couldn't breathe. I didn't know what to think. I tried to calm myself. I caressed my granddaughter's hair even as she seemed unsure of this. I shuddered and my hands shook a little. I hugged my granddaughter, Ming. Ming has grown up now.

Slowly, Nini turns to look at Ming sitting on the sofa.

SCENE 3

MING *(sitting on the sofa)* Seeing my Grandma now, I can remember many things. When I was a little girl, Grandma found me reading a school book in bed. I was in Year 6 then. Grandma said she wanted to share some stories with me, to be close to me. She asked me about school, then she told me a story. She told me the story of "The Age of Kalabendu". According to her story, Good fought against Evil in the age of Kalabendu and Evil came out the victor. I protested: how come it was Evil that won? I've read many stories where the good heroes always win. Grandma continued her story, ignoring my protest. I don't know why, but now I am reminded of the Kalabendu tale... *(Pause. Ming stands.)* When I had grown up, I heard a story too about my grandma. It happened early one morning in December 1965. People rushed into her house. They said nothing. Five men surrounded my grandma, who was boiling water in the kitchen. They took her outside and put her in a waiting truck. There were many people in that truck. They stared at my grandma saying nothing. Grandma was three months' pregnant with her first child. The truck sped to Bukit Duri prison. Grandma's husband disappeared never to be seen again. Half a year later, on July 20, 1966, a baby was born behind the prison walls. She would grow up to be my mother. She was given a beautiful name, Rachmanina, Rachma, my mother.

Blackout.

SCENE 4

Late afternoon – early evening. Nini enters her room. She fixes the kebaya she is wearing, making herself look presentable, then tidies the bed. Then she goes to the wardrobe and takes out a photo album, caresses the album, and then walks back to the bed and sits. Slowly she opens the album.

NINI Yes, I remember. Here.

As Nini turns the pages, slides of the photos – old brownish photos – are projected on a screen at the back of the stage. The photos are of some of her friends at Plantungan prison camp and of the activities of Gerakan Wanita Indonesia. As the photos appear on a screen at the back of the stage, the song 'Salam Harapan' ('Greeting of Hope') can be heard in the background.

> The morning sun rises
> like a blooming red flower,
> as the jasmine blossoms bloom.

A hopeful greeting to you, comrades.

Stay healthy and strong.

Like a mountain of rock

in the middle of the ocean,

Stand up straight

against the crashing waves!

Our boat will race onwards

until we reach the shore of our dreams.

NINI *(She looks back. She is a little unsteady, holding the photo album.)* I can remember that day. It was the 2nd October 1965. I arrived at the office earlier than usual to write letters for my organization. A few of my colleagues were already there. They were busy talking about the kidnapping and murder of the generals which they had heard on the radio. I was shocked and confused. We were all confused *(Nini stands still holding the photo album.)* The streets were empty, very quiet. Not a sound to be heard, only a strange silence. I saw only a few cars on the street, it felt very strange to me. I saw a couple of trucks out on the street driven by soldiers in uniform. *(Trembling, a little frightened. Nini sits down on the bed again.)* I was confused. I didn't know what was happening. That was the start of our life on the run. Every time we heard gossip, or news about our disappeared friends taken away or killed somewhere. *(Pause. Nini caresses the album. She calls for Ming.)*

Ming... Ming...! What time is it, child? *(Nini looks tired and starts coughing.)* Ming... Ming...! What time is it?? Ming... Where are you, child...? You've left me without saying. You've left Grandma by herself like this. *(exits)*

SCENE 5

Ming enters and looks around the room. Ming calls out and walks quickly to the bedroom.

MING Grandma.... Grandma ...! *(Nini enters through the bedroom door. Ming is standing there.)*

MING   Grandma is not asleep yet? You're looking better. That's good.

NINI *(sitting up in the bed)* Where have you been?

MING   I went to Auntie Rohaya's house. We discussed the plans for tomorrow. Grandma's friends are coming here tomorrow? Auntie Rohaya is helping contact them.

NINI   Thank you. So who will come tomorrow?

MING   Auntie Rohaya said, Sulahana, Makmin and Tarwih. Rohaya said that her nephew would fetch them from their houses and bring them here together.

NINI   Ah, no need to go and get them. They can still go by bus. Don't think we can't get about by ourselves anymore and have become dependent on others.

MING   Yes, Grandma. But it's okay if the young people help you occasionally, yes? They have to come from a long way. Tangerang, Bekasi and Cibubur.

NINI   What did Aunt Rohaya say? Did she have anything special to tell you?

MING   What do you mean, Gran?

NINI *(investigating)* Something special, not just asking how I was?

MING   Gran, can I ask something?

NINI   Hey, how come you are answering a question with a question? What do you want to ask?

MING   Have you ever been happy, Grandma? What are your recollections of when you were the happiest?

Nini gets up from her bed. She is restless and seems sad. She walks to the centre of the room. Ming stands up and just looks at Nini, confused.

MING   I'm sorry, Grandma. You don't have to answer me.

NINI   Ming, can you get the doll with the headband in my room?

Ming walks quickly to Nini's bedroom and brings back a doll, with its hair tied up by a headband. She hands it to Nini.

NINI Sit here near me, child. *(Ming moves closer to her grandmother.)* If this doll could speak, it would answer all your questions. So you really want to know whether Grandma has ever been happy? Why is that important for you?

MING I want Grandma to be happy.

NINI I've got one foot in the grave already, child. It's not important whether I am happy. And you, child, are you happy?

MING Ah, Grandma… It's like we're playing ping-pong with the questions.

Nini is silent for a moment. Then she speaks again while holding her doll. Then she attaches the doll's headband to Ming's hair.

NINI You are pretty like your mother, Ming.

MING Mother… I haven't spoken the word "mother" for such a long time. But Grandma is also my mother, yes?

Nini bows, sad. She holds her doll tightly.

NINI Perhaps it is time I told you everything, child. You have a right to know.

MING About your history? I already know, Grandma.

Nini is startled. She observes Ming's countenance carefully for several moments.

NINI Auntie Rohaya?

MING *(nods slowly)* Yes…

NINI Forgive your grandma, Ming. I always wanted to tell you everything. To be honest with you. I was afraid my story might drive you away from me.

MING Rohaya has told me a lot.

NINI Have I disappointed you? Are you ashamed? Or afraid? Now that you know who I really am?

MING I love you more than anything, Gran. Nothing can change that. Even while there are questions swirling around in my head. And the doll? Can I borrow the doll, Grandma? The doll is so beautiful.

Nini gives the doll to Ming. Nini observes Ming's face closely for some time.

NINI You are beautiful too. But your eyes – they remind me of your grandpa's. Ming, of course I have been happy. I have been very happy. The happiest moment was when I received the first poem from your grandpa...

MING Ah, Grandpa used to write poetry for Grandma? Ah, so romantic. But men who wrote poems like that are usually just flatterers, aren't they, Grandma?

NINI Oh no. Your grandpa was different! *(Then she laughs to herself. As if laughing at herself. Her face is happy.)* Your grandpa, Bung Daryo...

MING *(interrupting Nini)* Grandma calls Grandpa Bung? That's not romantic. You call your beloved one Bung?!

NINI Better than Bang. He was from East Java. If I called him Bang Dar people would think he was Betawi.

Nini and Ming burst into laughter together.

MING Why did you like Grandpa Daryo? Because he sent you poetry? Did Grandpa Bung Dar propose using poetry?

NINI When he proposed, he sent a very long letter. That was his proposal to me! I thought it was just going to be more poems as usual. There was no way I could give an answer right away. I mean, he proposed in a letter! From that moment on, his letters — sent from Jakarta — flowed like a torrent. I got to know him very well through his letters. Your grandpa was an artist. He was also active in politics. He liked music as well as poetry. He liked jazz as well as classical music. He could even play the piano. Sometimes, I also enjoyed listening to the music he would play at home. But I liked Lili Suryani best of all. She had a beautiful voice. So pure... *(She hums the words of the song.)*

MING You loved Grandpa, then?

NINI Who knows? We never used that word, love. But there was one thing he said that I always cherish.

MING What did he say, Grandma?

NINI "Keep smiling, my darling. Smile upon life!" Oh, Bung Dar...

MING Simple words, but full of meaning.

NINI Yes.

MING So how did you meet Bung Dar?

NINI We were both active in politics. I joined a women's organization in Solo. Bung Dar was in a cultural organization in Jakarta. We met during one of his visits to Solo. Those days all the young people were active in so many different things. We were all revelling in the glory of Indonesia. It was such a joy, the feeling of having your own country and being able to rule it yourself. We were no longer afraid of the Dutch. And the best thing was, we were doing all this together. We were doing all kinds of things: we built a daycare centre for children. We taught them how to read and write. Once, we even went out in the fields together to kill the rats that plagued the paddy-fields... In the end, we got married.

MING You married him in 1954, didn't you?

NINI Yes. Aunt Rohaya told you that, did she? Bung Dar took me to Jakarta. I became more active there. It was ten years before finally I was with child. We were very happy. We had decided on a name. We were sure the baby would be a girl. Bung Dar proposed the name: "Rachmanina". The name was a prayer, so that she might become a great pianist like Rachmaninoff, the famous Russian pianist. He had funny ideas sometimes, Bung Dar. But I went along with it – Rachma does sound nice, doesn't it? Just like an Indonesian name, but without the "-ninoff" at the end. So, Rachmanina, your mother.

Pause. Nini is sad. She takes the doll from Ming's lap. Nini embraces her doll and walks to her bed and sits down.

NINI Bung Dar never saw his own daughter. Your Grandpa just vanished after what happened at midnight on 30th September, 1965. I don't know, child. Even today I don't know what happened to him. Sometimes I think about how he might have died. But I feel he is still alive in my heart. *(Nini stops speaking for a moment, then speaks more slowly.)* Ming, Bung Dar was right: keep smiling. Smile upon life! That way we can get through all the sufferings and problems of life in an honest way and with a firm heart. Can you do that, Ming?

MING But, Grandma, I've always wanted to ask. Why do they always say that you and your friends danced naked? How can people accuse you and your friends of doing something as horrible as that? Why? I don't understand.

NINI I don't know, child. I don't know why and how that story was made up. But those lies really hurt me and all my friends. Imagine, suddenly people were calling us immoral women! *(While she speaks of Gerwani, photos of news clippings and other material containing dark propaganda against Gerwani are projected onto a screen at the back of the stage.)* The news spread so quickly to every corner of the country. Even now people still believe those lies. Those lies paralysed us. Even now, no one has ever denied those lies. You're not scared, are you, to hear or to say the word "Gerwani"?

MING I have to admit, it does feel strange in my mouth to say the word.

Nini stands.

NINI History is not always a fairy tale. But we have to learn about our own history, even the darkest parts of it, so we can understand our own life. Oh, tomorrow morning Grandma Sumilah will come for a visit.

MING Grandma Sum, she's coming too?
NINI You have to wake up early and help me.
MING Okay, Grandma.

Nini exits via bedroom door.

SCENE 6

After Nini exits, Ming is alone in the bedroom. She takes off her headband and puts it back on the doll. She walks slowly to the sofa, sits. The stage light shines on Ming.

MING Slowly I begin to understand who my grandma and my mother really are. My mother, who was given such a beautiful name by Grandma Nini and Grandpa – Rachmanina! Grandma dreamed that her daughter would grow up to be a great piano player like Rachmaninoff from Russia. A country that was close to my Grandma's generation. Who didn't admire the Soviet Union in those days? They represented hope for humanity, that's what I heard. They even gave their children almost-Russian names. But history chose its own course. Politics made things turn out differently. Millions suffered, including my grandparents and my mother.

Blackout.

SCENE 7

It is 8 o'clock in the morning. Sumilah sits at the dining table. She is by herself. She is wearing a skirt to her knees and a green, long-sleeved blouse. She has a white shawl over her shoulder. Her white hair is tied in a bun. She is wearing casual sandals. There is a bag on the floor by her feet.

SUMILAH I've always liked to dance. I started practising dance when I was 14, when the young people of the village started organizing classes. I enjoyed it so much. I felt free when I danced, so free and my spirit was full of joy. I felt free. Free!!! Then, a friend invited me to join volunteer training in Pasar Rebo. I can still remember. I was so proud to train as a volunteer. Do you know, the volunteers were invited by the president himself? I didn't know anything then. All I knew was we were to crush the imperialist puppet country of Malaysia! I wanted to join my friends. I was so proud.

At the Pasar Rebo Square we practised marching and drill, to get us disciplined, but we also sang songs and danced to boost our spirits and fight some of the boredom. Our trainers said it was also a way to keep our instincts sharp.

I grew to enjoy it there. We practised many different songs and dances. There was the well-known Jali-Jali. Keroncong Kemayoran, too. And my favourite: Genjer-Genjer! But the freedom I felt didn't last for very long.

(She hums the song Genjer-Genjer. It sounds cheerful. But she falls sad again and then continues her story.)

The flame of my youth only lit up briefly. I didn't have much time to enjoy my time as a young woman working hard for her country. Suddenly, everything turned into darkness and pain. *(Pause)*

The morning was still dark. Approaching dawn. All of us boys and girls were fast asleep after a day of training. Suddenly, armed soldiers raided our barracks. They shoved their rifles into our faces as we slept. It was the feeling of cold metal on my cheeks that made my eyes open, wide awake. I was staring right into the muzzle of a rifle. I was in shock. I didn't know what was happening.

Everybody started to panic. But no one knew what to do.

I remember clearly the shouts of the soldiers: "Devils! Whores! Sluts! You're the ones who cut up our Generals!" I became even more confused. Swearing at us and beating and hitting us, the soldiers forced us outside into the field. We could do nothing but obey their orders. We could feel the guns at our backs. They forced us to take off all our clothes. We stood there totally naked. Oh... what kind of a nightmare is this? For a moment, I felt the shame of seeing myself naked. *(She wraps her arms around her body. Frightened.)* I was shivering. They shouted at me. The morning air was brushing up against my neck and my whole naked body. I was confused: I felt disoriented. I was standing naked before these soldiers? Naked! Confusion quickly turned into a great fear. I began to shake. I was shivering with fear. *(She wraps her arms around her body again.)* I tried to cover my private parts and my breasts. I saw my friends all doing the same. I tried to lift up my head, but I was too afraid. I was so afraid at that moment. All I could do was bow my head.

(Pause. Sumilah sits. She trembles. She regains her composure, to feel strong again.)

We were kept in that field for two days, naked, with no food or water. The next day, I was summoned to the barracks where the soldiers were staying. I was interrogated repeatedly about what happened at midnight on the 30th September.

I didn't know what to answer. They were shouting and swearing at me non-stop. Then they pushed me outside when they couldn't get the answers they wanted.

But the next day, I was summoned again. I was shivering. I was ordered to get dressed. There were several interrogators in the room and also a man with a camera. I can still remember all their questions: Is it true that male and female volunteers held an orgy in front of the generals? Is it true that I performed the "Perfumed Flower" dance naked in front of the generals? And is it true that my friends and I then slashed the generals' private parts? And I was forced to answer "Yes" to all these questions.

When they got all the answers they wanted the soldiers stripped me naked again. I couldn't move, as if I was dead.

Each time they struck my body, I thought about my mother and the times I was learning to dance and sing together with the other young people in my village. The memories helped me forget the pain. Oh Lord…

(Pause. Sumilah bows her head. Sad. She trembles but is calm. She tries to sit up straight and rubs her face.)

SCENE 8

Nini and Ming enter.

MING *(walking towards Sumilah)* Grandma Sum…

Sumilah turns around to see Nini and Ming. Sumilah gets up and walks to Nini. They embrace. Ming watches.

NINI Jeng, how are you?

SUMILAH Ya, getting old, of course. And how are you, Mbakyu?

NINI Yes, the same. Getting older and older. *(laughing)* But you still look sprightly!

SUMILAH Really? *(looking pleased)*

Nini invites Sumilah, and then Ming, to sit down.

NINI Jeng, sit here. Ming, come sit with us. *(The three of them sit. A conversation starts.)* We haven't seen each other for a year, Jeng. The last time we met was when Ratmi passed away, yes?

SUMILAH Jeng Mia Sungkono passed away just a few months ago… you heard?

NINI Mia from Klaten? I didn't hear that? Was she ill?

SUMILAH Old age, what else? We're all getting old. We are all on our way. I rang here when Mia was dying, but I think Mbakyu Nini was ill herself then.

Grandma Nini coughs a little. She looks exhausted. Sumilah and Ming can see that Nini looks very tired.

SUMILAH Mbakyu Nini, you don't look well. You should rest…

MING You should sleep.

NINI Sleep? I have been waiting for Jeng Sum for such a long time. We haven't met for a year. I'd like to stay awake. I'm okay. *(To Ming)* Could you make some hot tea?

Nini coughs again. Ming goes out back. She returns later with two cups of tea.

SUMILAH If you want to lie down, we can still talk, Mbakyu. I don't mind.

NINI Look, I've done my hair, got all dressed up in kain and kebaya – how can I lie down now? I am alright, I'm fine. I miss you, Jeng Sum. We can exchange stories here. My granddaughter, Ming, needs to hear them too. You want to, don't you, Ming?

MING Of course, Grandma. The other guests will be here around three o'clock. Aunt Rohaya has organized them.

SUMILAH Who else is coming, Mbakyu?

NINI Ah, you'll find out later. A surprise! *(chuckles)* When I rang to ask you to come here last month, I hadn't thought of asking the others. We haven't met each other for such a long time. We only gather for a funeral when one of us dies.

NINI Do you remember the oath we used to recite at Plantungan?

SUMILAH The sufferings and difficulties which have befallen us will not shake the resolve of our spirits…

SUMILAH AND NINI *(together)* Our bodies may fall sick. Our hearts will stay strong and calm like the green trees that surround our camp. Our souls will loyally sing like the singing of the steady flow of the Plantungan river that sends its water to distant villages, no matter how many twists and turns it has to go through.

MING That is beautiful, Grandma.

NINI Beautiful? It was just a prayer to keep us strong and standing up straight. We had to accept what we were going through as an experience to be understood. Otherwise, these grandmothers of yours would have collapsed from the moment we were arrested and humiliated, just taken away with no chance to defend ourselves. *(To Sumilah)* You used to say that every morning, but still cry in the evenings…

SUMILAH Who didn't shed tears, Mbakyu? The pain and the humiliation — I've never felt anything worse. Such pain… *(laughs grimly)*

NINI Ming, are you ready to hear the tales of us old people? You might not enjoy them. Our stories might be a bit depressing.

MING So that's why Grandma has invited her friends here, to tell me stories?

NINI Not just for that. I miss my friends too. I don't know why, but I really wanted to see them all again. You don't mind, do you? To be with Gran and her friends?

MING Of course, I don't mind. *(Then she asks Sumilah, hesitantly)* Oh, can I ask you something, Grandma Sum? Are you…? Auntie Rohaya told me once about a fourteen-year-old girl who was imprisoned.

SUMILAH I am not going to repeat my tales of woe, Ming. I'm sorry. I'm tired. My head hurts.

MING Auntie Rohaya also told me about the "night receipts".

SUMILAH I told you I'm not going to...

NINI *(shaking, she interrupts Sumilah)* When it was time for the "night receipt", time stood still. Everyone was silent and afraid. Everybody would pray hard – who knows what they were praying for? Perhaps hoping that they wouldn't be taken, or that their friends who were taken would survive their ordeal. We were shaking...

SUMILAH Enough, Nini! Enough! Why do we keeping going over and over those terrible times?

NINI So that my granddaughter knows. So that the world knows...!

SUMILAH What's going to happen if the world knows about our suffering? Will anything change for us? We go over and over that barbarity, but can you really feel what I went through? You've never been molested, stripped naked, burnt with cigarette butts, electrocuted! Do you know how that feels?

NINI Well, do you know what it's like to deliver a baby in prison? Do you know what it's like to have a husband who disappeared without a trace, never to return home? Perhaps he was shot – I will never know.

Ming is confused and tries to calm Nini. She speaks slowly while stroking Nini's hand.

MING Enough. Enough now...

NINI Let it go, we're not trying to work out who has suffered the most. We must support each other. So we can stay strong. Stay strong and keep a smile on our faces. Remember our oath? What else can we do? Let it go. We are old now. I don't want to open old wounds, but my granddaughter must know these things. So her own life is not dragged down by her family's dark past. It's our responsibility to tell this story.

SUMILAH But, I can no longer... Sister... I'm sorry. Forgive me... I'm okay.

Nini coughs again. Sumilah tries to calm herself and wipes her tears with the corner of her blouse. Ming is silent. Suddenly Suminah embraces Suhartini. They cry while holding each other. Ming sits silently. Shocked and confused, she tries to remain calm. The two old women weep softly.

NINI Do you want to freshen up a bit now, maybe take a shower and change your clothes? You must be tired.

Nini and Sumilah walk off slowly, holding each other, their voices fading as they leave the stage.

SUMILAH I miss you, Mbakyu.
NINI I miss you, too.
SUMILAH I brought you something.
NINI Did you?
SUMILAH Your favourite.

Nini and Sumilah go off stage while Ming watches them.

SCENE 9

Ming is alone onstage, in the middle. The stage light focuses on Ming.

MING Now I know more about my grandmother's history. But I'm even more confused. I don't know how to deal with what I'm feeling now. Gran's other guests will be here soon. What will I hear next? Grandma wanted me to listen to all of their stories. She thinks it will help me deal with my own sadness and suffering, that I'll know I'm not alone...

Ming exits.

Blackout.

SCENE 10

Late afternoon. The stage is empty. Makmin and Tarwih enter the stage from a door at the back centre stage. Makmin has short hair, just down to her ears, and all her hair is white. She wears a simple, brown full-length dress and a green jacket. She wears flat shoes and black socks. She uses a cane to walk. Tarwih is wearing a brown kain and white kebaya. She still has vigour. They are happy to arrive at Nini's home.

MAKMIN When you're not well, old people like us, going somewhere isn't easy, but still I'm pleased. We made it here at last. Thanks to Rohaya for organizing to get us here. Hey, there's nobody here?

TARWIH Where's everyone?

Ming enters and greets the two women.

MING Good evening, all.

MAKMIN Ming?!

MING Yes, Grandma. And you are …? *(unsure)*

MAKMIN Grandma Makmin!

TARWIH I'm Grandma Tarwih, child.

MING Ah, Grandma Makmin and Grandma Tarwih. Oh, Grandma Sumilah is here, too. But Grandma Nini hasn't been well. She's still resting with Grandma Sumilah. I'll fetch them in a minute. *(She exits.)*

MAKMIN Last week when Rohaya called me, I asked about Mbakyu Nini, Rohaya told me Mbakyu Nini was fine.

Nini, is followed by Sumilah, then Ming enters. Makmin and Tarwih are very happy to see Nini and Sumilah. They exchange embraces.

MAKMIN *(as she embraces Nini)* Mbakyu Nini! Ah yes, you've got a bit of a temperature.

NINI *(to Ming)* I'll introduce you to all of my friends. This is Grandma Makmin. And this is Grandma Tarwih. You met them a few times when you were still a child.

MAKMIN She must've forgotten.

NINI We used to gather here as well.

MAKMIN But she was still so small then, sister. Now she's a big girl. Of course she's forgotten who we are. She even asked me what my name was!

NINI *(to all her friends)* Please, sit down.

They all move to the dining table. They sit down around the table. Ming exits. Before sitting down, they suddenly start singing. It is a song they all used to sing together in the Plantungan camp. Whenever they meet, as if keeping an unspoken promise, they sing this song as their anthem. After a few lines, they realize that not everybody has arrived yet.

ALL *(singing together)*
>The morning sun rises
>
>like a blooming red flower,
>
>as the jasmine blossoms bloom.
>
>A hopeful greeting…

MAKMIN Hang on, not all of us are here yet.

SUMILAH Ah, yes.

TARWIH Jeng Sum, when did you get here?

SUMILAH Me? I got here this morning, around eight o'clock.

MAKMIN Did you catch a bus?

SUMILAH No, I prefer the train.

NINI But, where is Jeng Hana?

MAKMIN Maybe she's on her way here. She said she had some errand to attend to. You know how us old women are.

NINI But she's coming, isn't she?

MAKMIN She said she wouldn't miss it. Don't worry. How are you doing? You've got a bit of a fever.

NINI I think I'm much better now. How are your children?

Ming brings in some drinks and places them on the table. She stands near to Nini.

MAKMIN Praise be to God, they're all good. Oh, and I have good news. Ranti, my youngest child, will be getting married soon.

(Hearing Makmin telling of her happiness that her daughter is getting married, Nini looks sad. Her head is bowed in sadness. She is reminded of Rachma. Makmin keeps on happily telling her story and laughing at herself, unaware of the change in Nini's countenance.) But me, I'm not so good these days. I get night sweats, back and forth to the loo, arthritis in my bones... the works. *(They laugh again.)*

NINI *(slow and sad)* If only Rachma was still alive...

TARWIH Let it go, Mbakyu...

MAKMIN I still remember your baby crying inside the camp. A lot of time has passed.

TARWIH Look at your granddaughter now, she's so beautiful.

Nini coughs. Ming offers her something to drink.

SUMILAH Do you want to go and lie down again?

NINI No, I prefer to be here.

Nini's guests enjoy their tea, and Nini offers them cakes. Nini sings Genjer-Genjer slowly and beautifully. All are quiet.

NINI *(singing Genjer-Genjer)*

Look at the genjer flowers on the rice fields...

A boy's mother comes to pick the genjer flowers...

SUMILAH This song always brings me back to happy times when I was young.

MAKMIN Who doesn't know this song?

NINI But times changed, that song became a curse to anyone who had ever sung it.

MING Why did they ban the song, Gran?

TARWIH They banned a lot of good things, child, and left a lot of bad things be. Those were the times, and they keep changing.

MING But I don't understand.

NINI Not everything can be understood right away.

The mood darkens. They are all suddenly silent.

MAKMIN Well, this is a bit grim, isn't it! Tell me some other news, I haven't seen all of you for so long!

NINI How come Jeng Hana isn't here yet?

MAKMIN Maybe she's got other things to do, that woman!

NINI *(to Ming)* Can you go out on the street and wait for Grandma Sulahana there?

Ming exits.

TARWIH Can I ask you something, does Ming know about…?

MAKMIN *(joining in quickly)* Rachma's brother? Have you told Ming about him? I'm sorry I have to ask you about this.

SUMILAH Yes, you told me that you want to tell Ming everything. Have you told Ming? Forgive us for asking. Maybe Ming needs to know, Mbakyu.

Nini has a coughing fit. She tries to get it under control.

NINI That's why I invited all of you here. You and Jeng Hana were closest to me – you understood what I was going through. *(She sobs. She wipes the tears with the corner of her kebaya.)*

MAKMIN That's why we're here today, too. This is not an ordinary reunion. We're here for you.

TARWIH We understand, this is not something that's easy to talk about. Especially when you have to tell your own granddaughter. We're here to give you strength.

NINI I really want to get rid of all those horrible memories. But I'm not sure if I can.

MAKMIN Sure you can.

SCENE 11

Sulahana suddenly enters with Ming. She walks with a walking stick in her right hand. The four women change the subject of their conversation and try to look cheerful. Sulahana looks fresh. She is wearing a brown kain and a blue kebaya. Her hair is white and in a neat bun. She has a colourful scarf and a bag.

SULAHANA I'm sorry I'm so late.

SUMILAH   How are you, Jeng? We thought you weren't coming.

MAKMIN   All of us are here now.

Sulahana, Nini, Makmin, Tarwih and Sumilah stand in a circle around the table. Ming stands observing her grandmother and her guests.

SULAHANA   Hang on. I'm ready now. One, two, three…

(Singing together)

> The morning sun rises,
> like a blooming red flower,
> as the jasmine blossom blooms.
> A hopeful greeting to you, comrades
> Stay healthy and strong
> Like a mountain of rock
> in the middle of the ocean,
> Stand up straight
> against the crashing waves!
> Our boat will race onwards
> until we reach the shore of our dreams.

They all sit.

MING *(admiringly)* So, did you all belong to the same organization?

SULAHANA   Each of us has our own tale to tell, our own experiences. Your grandmother was a real activist. So was Grandma Makmin and Tarwih. I was just a housewife who wanted to learn how to paint. That's why I often visited the house at Cidurian Street. That was where all the artists hung out at that time. But fate is never fair.

TARWIH   Fate brought us together unexpectedly. Behind bars, in exile, in torture chambers, even in isolation.

NINI C'mon, let's tell inspiring stories instead, my granddaughter is here. Tell stories that we can be proud of, don't just tell sad stories all the time.

SULAHANA Well, Ming, Grandma Makmin and Tarwih were an incredible duo then.

TARWIH Really. Really?

SULAHANA Seriously, others were cowering in fear, but these two were brave enough to make flyers.

MING What flyers?

MAKMIN The two of us were handing out pamphlets for the Sukarno Supporters Front, which was led by sister Lami and Jinah. They had the idea to spread these flyers to help Sukarno. I heard from Lami that because of what happened on the night of 30th September, some people were trying to get rid of Sukarno. Of course we were only too ready to help. All we had in mind was to help protect our President.

TARWIH But we were soon arrested. I only managed to hand out two flyers!

MAKMIN Of course we got arrested straight away. Tarwih did something very stupid. She didn't try to hide the flyers, even though they were banned.

TARWIH *(annoyed with Makmin)* That wasn't my fault! It wasn't because I put the flyers everywhere...

MAKMIN But you did...

TARWIH *(more annoyed still, defending herself and raising her voice)* It was because someone reported me to the authorities! As if you didn't know that was what happened. Do you know who reported me, Jeng?

SUMILAH Calm down, calm down.

TARWIH Jeng Makmin can be a strange one. She was always like that; I could never work out why...

MAKMIN Ah, quit it, don't get mad. Whatever happened we were always together, in prison! From Bukit Duri to Plantungan. Okay, I'm sorry, I apologize. But, it was true, someone told me...

TARWIH Why do you believe those people, those were just rumours...

SULAHANA Okay, quit it both of you. There's no use blaming each other. We're not here to fight about what happened in the past. Do you want to rest, Nini? *(turning to look at Nini who seems tired)*

NINI No, I'm okay. I want to stay.

SULAHANA If you think about it, we've lived a very long time. I'm 80 years old now. But what can we do now? Apart from taking care of what's left of our family. Sometimes I just feel so exhausted. But there's something that still rankles me now and then. Why have they forgotten about us, as if we never existed?

MAKMIN What else can we do, Jeng? We're lucky enough to have survived this long, to be able to breathe the air freely.

SUMILAH But Mbakyu Hana is right. As old as we are now, we still have to carry the stigma from those unfounded lies and accusations. Think about it, will we ever be able to die in peace?

TARWIH It is unjust.

SUMILAH Of course it is.

NINI Fair? That word is a luxury. There's no justice in this country, for people like us.

MING How could you get justice, Gran?

SULAHANA Ming, we are old. What can we possibly do? Sometimes, all I want is just to find Bung Barus and go where he has gone. But where is he?

NINI Maybe Bung Dar and Bung Barus are watching over us from up there.

MING Grandma Hana, did Bung Barus know my grandfather Bung Dar?

SULAHANA Your grandfather Bung Dar and my husband Bung Barus were friends from when they were young. They were both cultural activists. But then, they just disappeared. We don't know where they went. Did they disappear together, or each on his own, we'll never know.

MAKMIN Sometimes, when you think about it, life has thrown us a lot of curve balls.

SULAHANA But, even though we're old, can't we do something? We just wait for news of someone's death, then meet at the funeral, to gossip about whose turn it will be next.

NINI We've been at death's door since the first time we were dragged into prison, when they took us to Plantungan camp against our will. But still, we've been able to grow old together. We can still meet up here and breathe freely... *(turning to Ming)* Ming, all of us are here now. What are we going to do for dinner?

MING Okay, Gran. I will prepare it now. *(She goes to exit.)*

MAKMIN I'll help you prepare dinner, Ming.

Makmin walks off followed by Ming and then Sumilah and Tarwih.

SCENE 12

Nini and Sulahana are sitting alone at the table.

SULAHANA Jeng Nini, are you ready to tell Ming what you've told me over the phone? The time is right.

NINI I'm old and I can no longer keep this secret from the person closest to me – my own granddaughter.

SULAHANA I understand.

NINI *(standing up, nervous and sad)* For years, I've kept this story to myself. Jeng Hana, to tell you the truth, I wanted to tell all this to my Bung Dar. I miss him terribly. Sometimes, I can barely breathe, as if someone was crushing my chest. But if Bung Dar were to find out what happened, I don't know if he would still want to be with me. Would he still respect and love me?

SULAHANA Jeng Nini, listen to me. No one can deny his love for you. I knew him well, I knew how much he respected and loved you. Once, he admitted to me sheepishly that he had admired you since the first time you met in Solo. He told me that not long before he disappeared. He did.

NINI *(calling out slowly, sad and longingly)* Bung Dar... Jeng Hana, have you noticed how similar Ming's eyes are to Bung Dar's? Will I be able to tell Ming everything? I don't want Ming to get hurt, I don't want her to be upset, of course not. But I don't want to lie to her either.

SULAHANA It's hard. Tell you what, you're going to tell Ming the whole story after dinner. I know you've always been strong. And Ming is your granddaughter. It will be hard on her, she's still young. But I'm sure she will try to understand. She will learn how to be strong. We are all here to support you. Stay calm and everything will be okay.

Silence.

SCENE 13

Ming enters bringing food, followed by Makmin, Tarwih and Sumilah. Everybody is cheery. They sit at the table while Ming serves the food.

MING Dinner is ready.

TARWIH This is a lot of food.

SULAHANA Do you like to cook, Ming?

MING Not really, some of these dishes are takeaways.

SULAHANA When we were in Plantungan, all of us had to be able to cook. Anything edible around the camp, we'd cook up into meals.

SUMILAH We also had to learn how to plant vegetables in the garden.

MAKMIN Oh, and also how to catch fish in the rivers.

TARWIH Sometimes snakes, too! Do you remember the name of our friend, who used to cut up snakes to eat?

SUMILAH Darsinah?

MAKMIN No, not Darsinah.

TARWIH It sounds similar, though.

MAKMIN Ah, Dahmirah! She was very brave.

TARWIH   There was one time... that I will always remember...
SUMILAH   When?
TARWIH   Jeng Nini caused a huge commotion in the barracks...
MING   What did you do, Gran?
TARWIH   One morning, your grandmother went to pick vegetables in the garden in Plantungan. She found this plant that, if you put several in a row, can look like meat.
MAKMIN   That day, your grandmother had an idea. She only told us two. In the kitchen, she cooked everything up for our lunch that day. To convince everyone at the camp, your grandmother called out in front of the kitchen door. "Sisters, today I bought some meat from the market, so I've prepared a special dish for all of you. Just wait for it."
TARWIH   That's what she said, Ming. And then what happened? Everyone at the camp was so excited, they hadn't seen any meat for years! At lunch, there was a big commotion. Because the so-called meat turned out to be... tough! And it tasted strange. People worked out it wasn't actually meat.
TARWIH AND MAKMIN *(together)* It was a plant called "cockscombs". *(laughs)*

Nini drops her spoon. She says nothing and seems nervous. All her fiends watch her.

MING   Eat up, Gran. *(Nini says nothing and gazes at Ming.)* What's wrong, Gran?
NINI *(speaking slowly and deliberately)* Ming, now you've heard my stories, and the stories from my friends, do you still love me?
MING   What are you talking about, Gran?
NINI *(restless)*   Sorry, I have to go to the toilet.

Ming escorts Nini slowly off stage.

SUMILAH   Careful.
SULAHANA   Poor Nini!

Ming returns onstage.

MING	Grandma is not well tonight.
SULAHANA	Come here, Ming. *(Ming approaches Sulahana.)* Has your grandma ever told you anything else, apart from what you know about your mother and your grandfather?
MING	What do you mean, Grandma Hana?
SUMILAH	Ming, I think your grandma wants to tell you something.
MING	About what?
SUMILAH	I know your Grandma very well. She often finds it hard to speak of things that are important to her. Go and see how she is.

Ming goes back stage again to check on Nini.

SULAHANA	The secret that Jeng Nini is keeping from her granddaughter is torturing her.
SUMILAH	This morning Ming did ask me about the torture inside our prison. Then Mbakyu Nini and I had a bit of a fight.
SULAHANA	But why?
SUMILAH	Because I don't want to relive that story again.
TARWIH	No, it's never pleasant to go back over the ordeals we went through.
MAKMIN	But the important thing now is to work out how we can help Jeng Nini.
SULAHANA	I have a feeling Ming will understand; she's strong enough.
MAKMIN	I hope so.

Pause.

SCENE 14

Nini returns with Ming. As they approach the dinner table, Nini is not sure she wants to sit there.

NINI	I'm going to sit over there. *(pointing to the sofa)*
MING	Yes, Grandma.

Ming guides Nini to the sofa. Ming stands beside Nini who is sitting on the sofa. Her friends are all watching.

NINI　　　Do you ever think... or at least imagine that you might have another relative?

MING　　　What do you mean, Grandma? *(Nini glances towards the table.)*

NINI *(trying to remain calm)* Your mother, she had a brother.

MING　　　I don't know what you're talking about, Grandma.

NINI　　　I didn't only give birth to your mother in the prison. Forgive me, child. I couldn't tell you this before.

One morning, very early in the morning, I was summoned to the prison warden's room. He asked me to make him a meal. He'd prepared all the ingredients. I didn't have a bad feeling, no premonition. I set about my task, even though I was still sleepy. It was only past four o'clock then. The first thing I did was cook the rice. When I was about to wash the rice, the prison warden went into the kitchen. I didn't say anything. There was no need to talk.

I hadn't even finished washing the rice when he told me to tidy up his bedroom.

I felt scared then, but I couldn't say no. Carefully, I went into his bedroom. Despite my best efforts, I was powerless to resist him as he threatened me and put his hand over my mouth.

(Pause. Sulahana gets up, approaches Nini and sits beside her. Nini continues her story: her voice tense and strained.)

That was when he did something so evil that it has affected me more deeply than anything else since. It wasn't the last time he did it to me, either. He did it many times, threatening me if I tried to resist.

One time, because I couldn't stand it anymore, I was so ashamed, of myself, of the world around me, I almost ended it all. Jeng Hana saved my life. *(She cries a little, tense and strained.)* She reminded me that I still had Rachma, your mother.

(Nini tries to restore her calm.)

Ming, can you fetch me the doll and the hairband from the bed? The doll and the hairband, child.

Ming walks quickly to get the doll and headband from the bed and brings it back to Nini. Nini holds it in her lap. Sumilah, Tarwih and Makmin come across close to Nini.

SULAHANA Jeng Nini, all of us here are with you. Be strong.

NINI I got pregnant and gave birth to a son. I never wanted to see him. Seeing his innocent eyes reminded me of my ordeal. My friends took the baby to a family in the village near Plantungan. I didn't know what name they gave to my baby and I didn't want to know. Was I wrong to do that, Jeng Hana?

SULAHANA/ MAKMIN/ TARWIH/ SUMILAH
(*spontaneously together*) No.

NINI Am I in the wrong?

SULAHANA No.

NINI I didn't want to take care of that baby. But lately, I remember his eyes. I know that baby was born without sin. But then, Rachma's face and Bung Dar's face came to me, too. I can't get them out of my mind. *(Pause)* Come here, my child. Sit next to your grandma.

MING *(embracing Nini)* Why have you waited so long to tell me this, Gran?

NINI You've always asked me about this doll. *(caresses the doll.)* I made it myself in the Bukit Duri prison, a few days after Rachma, your mother, was picked up by her adopted mother. While sewing and making this doll, I used to pray that one day I would be able to meet Rachma again. I made this doll for your mother, child. I imagined that Rachma would grow her hair long, so I made her this hairband. She'd look even more beautiful when she put this hairband on.

Rachma... Rachma... My pretty... *(laughs but sad)* But... Rachma never saw this doll or her hairband. *(Pause)* All I ever heard were stories about that boy, oh how he grew up, stories I didn't want to hear at all...

MING Grandma, you're running a temperature again.

SUMILAH   Yes, Mbakyu Nini, you should rest. Take your Grandma to bed, Ming.

NINI   No, no, I want to stay here.

TARWIH   Please, have a rest, Jeng.

NINI   Sisters, I am relieved to have gotten all of this off my chest, to leave my soul easy. Maybe I'll soon get to see Bung Dar and Rachma.

ALL *(together)*   No, no. Don't say that.

NINI   My task here is finished. I have raised my granddaughter to be a grown woman. Haven't I, child?

ALL *(taking turns to speak, worried)* You're getting feverish. Lie down on the bed.

Her friends take Nini back to her bed. She sits on the bed embracing the doll.

NINI   Forgive me, my child, if I can't give you all the happiness you deserve.

You have to always remember what your grandfather once said, "Keep smiling, smile upon life!" If you do that, life will smile back at you. Don't be sad. Learn from all the tales of your grandmothers' past. Learn from our past.

Now, this doll is for you.

Nini gives the doll to Ming. Ming accepts it nervously and sadly. Ming walks slowly back to the sofa at the centre of the stage. Nini's friends slowly help her lie down. They stay there with her.

ALL   Come on, lie down.

SCENE 15

Ming sits on the sofa, embracing the doll.

MING   My grandmother has left me a legacy of a dark past. A dark past beyond her imagining. For years, she was forced to bury that past deep inside her soul. My grandmother sings songs of sadness, of loss, of wrongful accusations made in cruel silence. My grandmother had to suffer mental and physical pain inflicted by a power she could not fight. But I know, despite the pain, she was never broken. She raised her spirits with her hopes that her granddaughter could face the future with courage.

Grandma, I don't know what to do now. (*She looks across to Nini and her friends.*)

There is so much bitterness, but also relief. Because now I know your story. For years you have sung in silence, now your songs echo in every corner of my mind, finding their way into every pore of my skin.

(She stands, still holding the doll.)

Now I understand the meaning of the Kalabendu tale you once told me. Good doesn't always win, and not every tale has a happy ending. But everyone will keep on fighting, though good may not always prevail.

Grandma always said that virtue and honesty would help us understand our destiny, and our duty to be human.

I will always remember what you told me, Grandma – to keep smiling upon life, despite all the bitterness it brings, so we can stay strong and brave.

Dear Gran, I want to hold on to you tighter and tighter. I want to hug you again, even tighter this time.

Lights Out.

The End.

Glossary

Kebaya – Indonesian traditional blouse.

Gerwani – Gerakan Wanita Indonesia – Indonesian Women's Movement.

Jeng – A familiar term of address to a younger woman friend.

Mbakyu – A familiar term of address to an older woman friend.

Bung – A term of address to a male comrade.

Bang – A term of address for an older male brother, or an older male.

Kain – A wrap-around for the waist, worn by women, like a sarong.

Plantungan – a camp for female political prisoners associated with the Indonesian Communist Party (PKI) in Central Java.

Bukit Duri – a prison in Jakarta.

Genjer-Genjer – the title of a popular folk song in the years before 1965. It was banned under the Suharto government and was considered taboo and associated with the Indonesian Communist Party.

Faiza Mardzoeki

A playwright, theatre producer and director based in Yogyakarta, Indonesia. She actively promotes gender equality issues, human rights and other social issues through the arts. Since 2003, she has produced fourteen plays, as well as two concerts and been the initiator-executive director of two major arts festivals. As well as producing theatre, she has written or adapted ten plays, including her critically acclaimed *The Silent Song of the Genjer Flowers*, which has been performed in Jakarta, Indonesia and screened in venues in the United States, Netherlands, Australia, Malaysia and Singapore. She also directed *The Silent Song of the Genjer Flowers*.

In July 2019, she received a grant from New York Foundation of the Arts to support her adaptation of her play *The The Silent Song of the Genjer Flowers* into a novel. In 2018, NORLA subsidized her Indonesian translation of *Time Without Books* by Norwegian playwright Lene Therese Tiegen. Faiza has also adapted the novel *Max Havelaar* by Dutch writer Douwes Dekker, into a stage play entitled *Mulatuli Meets Saidjah and Adinda* and two works by Henrik Ibsen, *Doll's House* and *Enemy of the People,* for the Indonesian stage.

She adapted Pramoedya Ananta Toer's epic novel, *This Earth of Mankind,* to a play titled *Nyai Ontosoroh* which was declared the iconic production of the year by

Kompas. The production which she also directed, toured to Amsterdam, The Hague and Antwerp, commissioned by Troppen Theater, Amsterdam.

She has participated and spoken at feminist and theatre-related events all over the world. Her play *The Silent Song of the Genjer Flowers* was selected for a dramatic reading at the Women's International Playwrights Conference in Santiago, Chile, October, 2018. www.faizamardzoeki.com

Gratiagusti Chananya Rompas

Gratiagusti Chananya Rompas began her writing career by establishing an online poetry collective called Komunitas BungaMatahari in 2000. Now, she is one of the organisers of Paviliun Puisi, a monthly poetry open mic in Jakarta. Her second book of poetry, *Non-Spesifik*, is now being translated into English with support from the Emerging Translators Mentorship 2018-19 program, organised by the National Centre of Writing in Norwich, UK. She received Honourable Mention from the 2018 Hawker Prize for Southeast Asian Poetry. She is a WrICE (Writers Immersion and Cultural Exchange) Fellow in 2018 as part of a residency program organised by RMIT University and has received a travelling grant to Scotland from Indonesia's National Book Committee and the Ministry of Education and Culture through the Indonesian Writing Residency 2018 program. Her latest works are upcoming in two anthologies, *The Near and the Far: Volume 2* by Scribe Publications and *On Relationships* by 3 of Cups. She writes both in Indonesian and English.

Mikael Johani

Mikael is a poet, critic, and translator from Jakarta, Indonesia. His works have been published in *Asymptote, The Johannesburg Review of Books, AJAR* (Hanoi), *Vice Indonesia, Kerja Tangan* (Kuala Lumpur), *Murmur, Selatan, Popteori, Vita Traductiva* (Montréal), *What's Poetry?, Bung!,* and others. His poetry book, *We Are Nowhere And It's Wow,* was published by Post Press in 2017. He's working on *mongrelz*, his second poetry collection, which will feature mostly codeswitching poems. He's also working on a translation of Gratiagusti Chananya Rompas's poetry collection, *Non-Spesifik*. His English version of *one by one the bodies died*, a poem from Non-Spesifik, won an Honourable Mention from the 2018 Hawker Prize for Southeast Asian Poetry. He is one of the winners of the 2018-19 Emerging Translator Mentorships Programme from the UK's National Centre for Writing in Norwich. He organizes Paviliun Puisi, a monthly open mic gig in Jakarta. His latest works are upcoming in *On Relationships*, an anthology published by 3 of Cups in the UK.

Playwright's Note:

The following story is about the uncovering of the mass graves of the victims of Gestokin in the village of Masean, in Batuagung in Jembrana in Bali, on 29th October 2015.

After a period of 50 years, a mass grave was uncovered in accordance with traditional practices. The act was a long time in the making, and in the ceremony, the corpses were purified and re-buried in the appropriate manner. It took so long, not because of politics, revenge or unhealed wounds, but more so due to a lack of funds. Balinese funerals (*ngaben*) are very expensive – especially so for "unusual deaths".

The mass grave was directly in front of the State Primary School No. 3 of Batuagung. There was no indication that there was a mass grave there. There wasn't even a pile of dirt. There was no garden or an old well, which were often used. The mass grave lay beneath an asphalted road.

A *ngaben* ceremony was performed for every skull that was removed. There were eleven victims buried in six shallow graves. Two victims couldn't be identified. They were presumed to have come from outside of the village. It was stated that the ceremonies were performed to remove the cosmic disturbances that were a result of the presence of corpses which had been buried inappropriately and not in the right place.

A funding campaign had enabled the exhumation of the mass grave. Money was sourced through volunteers and donations from various sources, including politicians, officials, businesspeople, netizens and various religious figures, most of whom were born after 1965. The uncovering of the grave was carried out without tears, grief and revenge.

But, in my play, it wasn't so for Srengi.

RED JANGER

Ibed Surgana Yuga

Translated by Andy Fuller
Editor: Kumiko Mendl

Characters

SRENGI about 70 years old
SUANA Srengi's husband. About 3-5 years younger than Srengi
YOUNG SRENGI Srengi before and around the time of 1965
TWO HEADLESS GHOSTS men, about 40 years old at the time of their killing
ALIT a girl in Grade 5 of Primary School, the daughter of Dura and Arini
DURA the son of Srengi and Suana, about 40 years old
ARINI Dura's wife, about five years younger than Dura
VILLAGE LEADER a man
OTHERS

Setting

A small village is suggested within a house. It's located in the region of Jembrana, Bali, to the south of a mountain range which divides Bali from the west to east.

Inside the house there is an old bed and a dirty, worn-out mattress on the cement floor. There is a small, old television. There are three bamboo cages with three roosters inside. Everything is messy. Cardboard, chairs, packets of children's food and school books lie all over the place. There are photos of celebrities from the 1990s on the wall, and a photo of President Suharto is peeling and all that can be seen is his name and his jacket. On other parts of the wall are posters for the No. 2 candidate for mayor and his running partner. There is the slogan, "Developing Jembrana from the Village Up".

A poorly paved road breaks through the house. By the sides of the road: a building of State Primary School No. 3 of Batuagung, a banyan tree with a small Balinese Hindu shrine beneath its leaves.

There is a kitchen in the house as well: some kitchen equipment, a gas stove with an LPG gas cylinder (government benefits for the poor), and a wooden stove that has been lit.

A shadow of an excavator appears on the old brick wall of the house.

PART 1

An excited crowd watch a cockfight on the road. The old bed is shaking while Suana is sleeping. Srengi is dreaming. Beneath the banyan tree, the Young Srengi is practising a Janger dance. She is dancing passionately and with all the allure of a star of the stage.

A rooster is defeated in the fight. The crowd erupts. Young Srengi is caught off-guard and her dancing ends. Srengi is exhausted and she sits silently. She walks over to the wooden stove and boils some water. The cockfight disappears gradually.

A pair of Headless Ghosts appear beneath the banyan tree, talking while laughing.

HEADLESS GHOST 1 He-he-he-he. You don't have a head.

HEADLESS GHOST 2 You too. It's just like yesterday. He-he-he-he.

HEADLESS GHOST 1 It means we are still the same.

HEADLESS GHOST 2 We're still friends.

HEADLESS GHOST 1 In the same position, with the same fate.

HEADLESS GHOST 2 We're still here.

They laugh at each other and themselves. Then they start to sing about their headless bodies and make small dancing movements.

Srengi makes a coffee, rolls a cigarette and lights it (trying to get rid of her anxiety).

HEADLESS GHOST 1 But I once had a head.
HEADLESS GHOST 2 Me too.
HEADLESS GHOST 1 It was cut off.
HEADLESS GHOST 2 Mine too.
HEADLESS GHOST 1 It has disappeared.
HEADLESS GHOST 2 Maybe a dog ran off with it.
HEADLESS GHOST 1 It's been fifty years.
HEADLESS GHOST 2 Half a century without a head. Hehehehe.

The two of them laugh again. They sing humorously and lightly.

Dura enters the house, looks tired, wears a t-shirt of the mayoral candidate with the No. 2 on it.

SRENGI	Where have you been?
DURA	On the campaign.
SRENGI	Why bother?

DURA *(drinking the coffee made by Srengi)* He's a good candidate.

SRENGI It's always been like that. All of them have all been good. But, look, our life doesn't change.

DURA This is different. Throughout the campaign period my expenses are covered. Petrol costs, money for food, cigarette costs.

SRENGI It is better to look after the farm. Don't get mixed up in campaigns. Politics is no different from cockfighting. It's more common to lose than to win. Even if you win, the money quickly disappears.

DURA This isn't gambling. Don't compare them. You're so old-fashioned.

SRENGI Yes, I am. I'm from another era.

DURA Dad is the one who keeps going to the cockfighting – try telling him.

Dura lies down on a thin mattress on the floor where his wife and two children are already asleep. The Headless Ghosts walk off down the road.

A rooster crows and then other roosters start to crow too. It's just gone midnight.

PART 2

Smoke drifts from the wooden stove. Srengi is cooking. Arini is breastfeeding her child in a corner of the house.

A few primary school children are singing the Janger song. Some of the children dance to the rhythm of the song. Alit is one of the children in the group.

Song:

> Jangi janger
> Sengsenge sengseng janger
> Sengsenge sengseng janger
> Serere Nyoman ngeyorin
> Kelap-kelap ngalap bunga
> Langsing lanjar pamulune nyandat gading
> Jalan jani majangeran
> Seriang ngentur rota roti
> Arasijang jangi janger
> Arasijang jangi janger[1]

Alit enters the house while still singing the song.

SRENGI	ALIT! Don't sing that song!
ALIT	Why not, Grandma?
SRENGI	Just don't sing that song.

---

1. There are many versions of the Janger song. The one above is just one of them. The song's lyrics are mostly a play on voices, so the words have little meaning. The song above tells of a girl named Nyoman, who is dancing Janger

ALIT	My teacher taught it to me.
SRENGI	Sing another song.
ALIT	It's for a performance.
SRENGI	You don't need to get involved in such things.

Alit is on the brink of tears and runs towards Arini. She hugs her mother and presses her face against her mother, trying to hide her crying. Arini comforts her. Dura comes over.

DURA	What's up?
SRENGI	Don't let your daughter sing that song.
DURA	Which song?
SRENGI	That song.
ARINI	Janger.
DURA	What's wrong with it? She's learning how to sing.
SRENGI	My ears hurt.
DURA	It's because you're old.
SRENGI	Don't let her join in the performances. There is no point. We are not an artistic family. Just study hard and don't get mixed up in any funny business.
DURA	You're strange, Mother.
SRENGI	So what? I'm just a strange, old person.

Dura turns on the television and starts watching a local TV station. The news item is about the election of the mayor in December 2015. The images are blurred; there are only sounds. Dura hits the television a few times, hoping to fix it. The picture appears for a moment, only to disappear again. It flickers on and off several times.

DURA	Bloody TV!

The following news is about the uncovering of the mass graves of the victims of the 1965 massacre in the village of Masean, in Jembrana in Bali, on 29th October 2015. A ngaben ceremony was performed for every skull that was removed. There were eleven victims buried in six shallow graves. Two victims couldn't be identified. They were presumed to have come from outside of the village. It was stated that the ceremonies were performed to remove the cosmic disturbances that were a result of the presence of corpses which had been buried inappropriately and not in the right place.

DURA Wow! It's on TV. Incredible! *(Pause.)* Bloody TV!

Dura hits the television again. Sometimes an image of a massive grave appears, which is a poorly paved road in front of the State School No. 3 of Batuagung. There are interviews with various elders.

While cooking and looking after the fire, Srengi listens to the TV news report. Her movements slow down in order to pay more attention to the story. Her face gives off a strange expression.

SRENGI So, it will be dug up?

The question isn't directed to anyone in particular. But Dura answers it, all the while frowning, as the TV still isn't working properly.

DURA Yes, that's right. The committee was formed by the village council.

ARINI How many were buried there?

DURA Apparently, there were eleven. Bloody TV!

ARINI Who are they?

Suddenly the pot Srengi is holding falls to the floor; rice goes everywhere and the boiling water spills.

The shadow of the excavator flickers.

PART 3

A pair of Headless Ghosts are talking beneath the banyan tree. Alit is reading her Indonesian for Grade 5 of Primary School book while lying face down on the floor.

HEADLESS GHOST 1 Our grave is being dug up.

HEADLESS GHOST 2 Is that good news or bad news?

HEADLESS GHOST 1 I hope our heads are found.

HEADLESS GHOST 2 Are you confident? Even our own bodies can't find our heads – let alone other people.

HEADLESS GHOST 1 Our poor heads, they'll miss out on being given a ceremony. They won't be able to join us in heaven.

HEADLESS GHOST 2 Are you sure we are able to go to heaven?

HEADLESS GHOST 1 Apparently, commies[2] definitely go to heaven. Hahahaha…

HEADLESS GHOST 2 Will the person who cut off our heads participate in the digging up? Because he'll know where our heads are.

HEADLESS GHOST 1 Have you forgotten? We have already hung him on his own farm.

HEADLESS GHOST 2 That was the one who cut *your* head off.

HEADLESS GHOST 1 Oh, was it? Why didn't I ask him about my head before I hung him? I'm so stupid. *(He taps the side of where his head would have been; so, he just taps an empty void.)* The person who cut your head off disappeared to Borneo, didn't he?

HEADLESS GHOST 2 It might have been him. Or someone else. I didn't get a proper look at him. My head was cut off from behind.

HEADLESS GHOST 1 Apparently, he went crazy and died after being hit by a truck.

HEADLESS GHOST 2 I'd love to go to Borneo to take my revenge. Even just against his spirit.

HEADLESS GHOST 1 After our grave has been dug up and our bodies have been given the proper ceremonies, we'll be free to go anywhere. We'll be able to visit the Lord Shiva's Palace, let alone go to Borneo.

HEADLESS GHOST 2 Enough of such talk. Let's go for a wander.

HEADLESS GHOST 1 Where to? We can't go beyond the temple in the north and the river in the south. We've already been everywhere around here.

HEADLESS GHOST 2 Let's do some more exploring. Let's imagine it as a new place that we haven't ever been to before. Have you ever been to Kuta? There are lots of naked foreigners there.

---

2. *Kaum merah*, means "red people", the members of the Communist Party of Indonesia.

HEADLESS GHOST 1 Are you sure? How would you know?

HEADLESS GHOST 2 From those young guys.

HEADLESS GHOST 1 Which young guys?

HEADLESS GHOST 2 The ones who get drunk by the side of the road, late at night.

HEADLESS GHOST 1 The ones who like to piss on our graves?

HEADLESS GHOST 2 Yes. I heard that there are lots of foreigners in Kuta who like lying around naked in the sun. Times have changed. Come on, let's go for a wander and think about Kuta.

HEADLESS GHOST 1 Okay, sure! Let's go.

HEADLESS GHOST 2 Just a moment... I've forgotten my hat. *(He turns back to the banyan tree and takes his hat.)*

HEADLESS GHOST 1 I'm quite surprised ... you've lost your head, but you still don't forget your hat.

HEADLESS GHOST 2 *(While wearing his hat on top of his neck)* It's good for protecting the wound on my neck. It's painful sometimes when the cold night air blows. Come on!

HEADLESS GHOST 1 But we really must go to Kuta after our bodies have been through the blessing.

HEADLESS GHOST 2 Yes, of course.

Then they walk along the road, singing about their heads. They sing about Kuta, where there are plenty of foreigners sunbathing in the nude.

Alit has fallen asleep on the floor, still holding on to the book that she had been reading.

PART 4

Srengi and Suana are talking underneath the bed. They are sitting with their backs to each other. On the bed, the Young Srengi is dancing with a small dagger. She dances a sacrifice dance.

In a corner of the house, Arini is trying to put her baby to sleep, singing a lullaby.

SRENGI You remember, don't you? I held the *ngaben* cremation ceremony for him before we decided to get married. I did it without digging up his grave.

SUANA Yes, of course I remember. I agreed that you should do the *ngaben* ceremony.

SRENGI And now they want to dig up these graves.

SUANA Just let them. Why not? Don't you want those memories to be dug up again?

Srengi quiets down for a moment.

The Young Srengi puts the dagger between her teeth. She then dances with it.

SRENGI It's already been fifty years. I still can't come to terms with my feelings. That whole event... I can't really talk about it even now...

SUANA Are you afraid?

SRENGI Not at all.

SUANA Do you regret anything?

SRENGI Nothing. I don't regret anything. But I curse that bloody event. That whole bloody year. That song... that dancing...

Srengi starts to cry, but she brings herself under control.

SUANA Do you hate that song?

SRENGI To hell with that song. But I like it... those sharp notes... And now our granddaughter is singing it. I don't want those melodies or that dance to become a part of her.

Suddenly the baby cries. Arini tries again to put her child to sleep while softly singing the Janger song. The Young Srengi dances a fragment of the Janger dance on her bed, holding the dagger as if it were a fan, seeming to follow the rhythm being sung by Arini.

SUANA Do you still love him?

SRENGI Of course, I do. But what is the point in loving a corpse?

SUANA You told me you loved him.

SRENGI	We're old already. He's in the ground. You're still alive.
SUANA	And you too?
SRENGI	Me? I've been living between life and death for fifty years.

PART 5

The television is on. It flickers on and off continuously. There are some news reports about the election of the mayor in December 2015.

Dura appears on the road, holding a bunch of posters for the No. 2 candidate for mayor. Dura walks towards the banyan tree and sticks three posters on the trunk.

Srengi cuts some vegetables in the kitchen and prepares the spices. Suana is bathing his three roosters. Dura arrives home and gives some leaflets of the candidate for mayor to his parents.

DURA Don't forget to vote for this one. Just remember his face.

SRENGI Your father isn't interested in voting.

DURA Why has he never voted?

SRENGI He's had enough, apparently.

DURA You're missing out if you don't vote. I'm on the campaign team. Make me a coffee, Mum? *(Srengi makes a coffee and gives it to Dura.)* Just make sure that Mum and Dad choose him. Number Two.

SUANA What has to be chosen?

DURA That one! Those leaflets I gave you earlier. He's got good ideas.

SUANA Like what? Thousands of mayors have come and gone, but the roads aren't getting any better.

DURA If he wins, he has promised that the road here will be tarmacked. *(He finishes his coffee quickly, lights a cigarette and then gets up to leave. Then he talks while walking out the* *door, carrying posters.)* Right, that's it, I'm going out to put the rest of these posters up. I'll be embarrassed if my own parents don't vote for him. It's hard enough to find supporters within one's own family, let alone others.

There is silence until Dura disappears.

SRENGI I've never asked your reasons for not wanting to vote.

SUANA After the massacre I swore I would never vote again.

SRENGI That's strange.

SUANA No, not really.

SRENGI You weren't involved in the same way I was. You were still too young at that time.

SUANA It doesn't depend on how old you were or to what degree you were involved. You are a woman. You don't know what went on in that schoolyard.

SRENGI But it is because I am a woman that I curse that event.

SUANA But it is because I am a man that I know exactly what went on. There weren't any women around.

SRENGI Yes… That's right. There weren't any women in the schoolyard. That's where all the men were slaughtered – including my husband. While women like myself were abused in the streets.

SUANA Yes… you've just gone on hearsay. You don't know exactly what happened in the schoolyard.

SRENGI Hearsay? That was a kind of terror. We were slandered. They said I was a crazy prima donna. A star of the stage who had lost her mind. A commie whore. A witch. I was blamed for all the sins in the village.

SUANA It was the era that made us so wild.

SRENGI They killed my husband in the schoolyard. They just buried him by the side of the road.

SUANA Who are you talking about?

SRENGI Who do you think? I'm talking about the nationalists[3]? The military?

SUANA Even after fifty years you don't know who killed him.

SRENGI Well, who else could it be?

SUANA You just believe what you hear on the TV...

SRENGI What do you mean?

SUANA Our village is not like the city... It's not like Jakarta. There was no military here to do the killing.

SRENGI Then who was it?

SUANA It was the commies who killed fellow commies. They did it because they were ordered to do it.

SRENGI Stop making things up.

SUANA The nationalists and the military are the ones who are lying. They just cut off the heads of two people who had come from another village.

SRENGI I saw them both. They were paraded in front of me, after I was stripped naked to see if I had the tattoo of the hammer and sickle on my thigh.

SUANA Do you know how many members of the National Party were in the village at the time? No more than ten per cent of us. They weren't brave enough to kill anyone. Us reds were ordered to kill fellow reds. The senior commies were brought out, one by one, from the school building. Then, hundreds of us were ordered to beat them up until they were dead. If we refused, we would be killed. The nationalists and military just watched.

SRENGI *(taken aback, shocked)* So... you mean... you were one of the men who killed my husband?

PART 6

Young Srengi is screaming and shouting wildly on the street. She is walking back and forth, holding a knife and threatening anyone

---

3. *Kaum item*, means "black people", the members of the Indonesian National Party

nearby. However, she is not threatening them with the blade, but with the handle.

An excited crowd watch a cockfight on the road. But it is silent. Suana is amongst the people who are involved in the cockfight.

The shadow of an excavator appears on the wall of the house.

YOUNG SRENGI

> Time has made this village go wild.
> I'm a savage.
> These hands will do anything.
> This mouth will say anything.
> These feet are crazy.
> This body has lost control.
> Go on, stab this depraved woman.
> Stab me!
> Kill me!
> Kill me!

Young Srengi goes to the corners and empty spaces, still with a knife and threatening, imagining there is somebody who wants to stab her.

Meanwhile, the sound of the cockfight's crowd is heard gradually, louder and louder, chiming in with Young Srengi's voice, then reaching a climax before stopping suddenly.

PART 7

Alit is walking by herself along the street. She is coming home from school and singing the Janger song while dancing. She doesn't look like she is alone, but as if there are others accompanying her. She arrives at a banyan tree and stops for a moment. She waves towards the banyan tree, as if she is accompanying some friends to their home. Then she leaves. She doesn't sing the Janger song anymore. Perhaps she is scared of being told off by her grandmother.

PART 8

Suana has come home from the cockfight. He is carrying an empty rattan cage. His rooster lost the fight.

Srengi is cooking. The stove is on.

SRENGI Did you lose?

SUANA When have I ever won?

SRENGI Then what is the point of it all, if you are always losing? It's nothing but entertainment.

SUANA Entertainment? I don't need entertainment. I don't need to gamble. I have never gambled on anything. You can ask the gamblers whether or not I have ever gambled.

SRENGI So, what's the point of it?

Suana is silent.

SUANA When I was young, I was never involved in cockfighting. But, after the massacre, I got interested.

SRENGI As a means of escaping?

SUANA That event set it off. After I had been forced to kill my own relatives and neighbours... I felt that we are all just manipulated into fighting... just like those roosters. Who knows why, but, ever since then, I have enjoyed watching the cockfighting. Just watching is enough, I don't need to gamble.

SRENGI And you've never voted again, either?

SUANA There's no point in choosing to lose.

Dura enters the house. He is wearing the t-shirt of the No. 2 candidate for mayor. He's carrying a flag and a bamboo flagpole. He puts the flag up on the pole and goes to leave.

SRENGI Where are you going?

DURA To the city. For the campaign.

SRENGI Don't bother with all this. What do you get from it?

DURA I'm part of the committee. This is the best candidate. I get money for cigarettes, petrol and food...

SUANA	And defeat.
DURA	What do you mean? This guy will definitely win.
SUANA	You don't understand. He might win, but you will still lose. Politics is just like cockfighting and you're just a chicken.
DURA	What do you know about politics, Dad? You don't even bother to vote.

Dura gets on his motorbike and revs it a few times and leaves.

Srengi stares at Suana. Then the melody of Janger echoes in her ears.

PART 9

The Village Leader is giving a speech in the road.

Srengi is sitting down smoking a hand-rolled cigarette near the stove, as if she is listening to the speech.

Beneath the banyan tree, the pair of Headless Ghosts are having a relaxed conversation. It is not clear what they are talking about, but now and then they are laughing.

VILLAGE LEADER Based on statistics in this district, the local suicide rate is very high. This figure doesn't include the numbers of unusual deaths. There have also been a few cases of people saying that they have been disturbed by headless ghosts. Our children, who are doing their best to study hard at school, have had inexplicable accidents, and some have been possessed by spirits.

All of this indicates that there is a cosmic imbalance. Our village is in a polluted state. The senior religious figures and respected elders of the village have often reminded us that the reason for this is the presence of a mass grave in front of the school for the victims of the Gestok – the 1965 massacre. These bodies aren't in the place that they should be; after all, this is not a cemetery. When something is in the wrong place, it will always cause a disturbance.

Even though in the past, their families held a ceremony for them, the village elders believe that it is necessary to hold a mass cremation ceremony as a means of cleansing and purifying the village. Based on the information that we have, there are eleven corpses buried there. Nine of the corpses come from this village. We don't know where the other two come from, so it is impossible to trace their families.

The purpose of digging up the grave is not to re-open old wounds. It absolutely isn't. There is no point in us trying to find out who was right and who was in the wrong. Our task now is to find out how we can cleanse this village from corpses that have been buried in the wrong place. We need to give them the proper ceremony, in accordance with our Balinese Hindu traditions.

We need to remember that the funds for this come from various sources – including people from our own village. We will also hold cockfighting events for a week in order to raise funds. The committee will also look for funds from various leaders, politicians and businessmen. We are very grateful that we have been provided with an excavator by the honourable chairman of the city council, so that the process of digging up the mass grave can happen fairly quickly. Furthermore, we need to....

The village leader continues his speech, but he can no longer be heard. All that can be heard is the sound of two Headless Ghosts talking beneath the banyan tree. They are lazing about, leaning against the trunk of the tree.

HEADLESS GHOST 1 They haven't been able to find our families. They don't even know where we come from.

HEADLESS GHOST 2 It's not important. I'm not even sure that my family remembers me.

HEADLESS GHOST 1 That's true. I think my family has also forgotten me.

HEADLESS GHOST 2 We've just got to accept it. We've been forgotten.

HEADLESS GHOST 1 Do you think they forgot us, on purpose?

HEADLESS GHOST 2 Who knows?

HEADLESS GHOST 1 But I do miss my child. He's probably old already.

HEADLESS GHOST 2 Yes… older than you. Our bodies haven't aged for fifty years. It's good, huh?

HEADLESS GHOST 1 When I left home, he had just started to learn to walk. I remember how he would chase me and then fall over in the front yard. I was on the road and his mother would pick him up and carry him. He would start to cry as I walked away…

PART 10

As usual, the stove is burning. Srengi is cooking. Suana is bathing his rooster.

The sound of a motorbike. Dura enters, with his hands on his head. He is bleeding.

Srengi is taken aback at the sight of her son.

SRENGI What happened?

DURA We had a fight with the supporters of Number One.

SRENGI Like I said, you shouldn't have got mixed up in all of this.

DURA They started it.

Suana just looks on as Srengi helps Dura take off his t-shirt, which is covered in blood. She then starts to dress the wound on his head.

SUANA *(mumbling)* We're nothing but chickens who always lose.

PART 11

The scene is the same as before. The stove is burning. Srengi is cooking. Suana is bathing his rooster.

In the corner of the house, Arini takes off her husband's bandage and puts some ointment on his wound.

In another corner of the house, Alit is talking with the pair of Headless Ghosts. It is unclear what they're talking about. But, from their movements, it seems as if they're singing the Janger song. Sometimes Alit starts to do the dance, while being led by the Headless Ghosts.

Srengi and Suana ignore each other while being occupied with their own tasks. But they don't seem to be focused on what they're doing.

SRENGI After the event, my husband once visited me in a dream. He told me that I could get married again if I wanted to. But at that time, I wasn't thinking about getting married. I was just thinking about dying. I was just waiting for them to come and pick me up, drag me away. For them to abuse me and call me a commie whore. And then they would kill me. How beautiful that would be.

Srengi gets up and goes over to the old bed, taking something from under the mattress. Suana looks up and sees Srengi is holding a small dagger.

SUANA You still have it?

SRENGI Yes.

SUANA I thought you'd thrown it away. You lied. You deceived me.

SRENGI You just asked me to throw it away. But yes, I'm sorry. I wasn't able to.

SUANA What's more, you kept it beneath our mattress. In our bed. The bed that I made myself for our marriage.

Suana's face is riddled with disappointment. Srengi's expression changes as she looks at the dagger. She walks over to the stove. Suana walks over to the bed, still holding his rooster. He stands on the bed. Srengi stands over the stove.

SRENGI Please forgive me. All this time, we've been sleeping on top of this dagger. We've made love on top of this dagger. But, until now, there hasn't been anyone who has been able to stab my body with it. Bloody hell!

Srengi starts to dance with the dagger over the stove. Her expression becomes fiercer and fiercer. It is as if she is holding back her desire for revenge. As if she is coming to terms with defeat.

At the same time, Alit gets more involved in dancing the Janger with the two Headless Ghosts.

Meanwhile, Arini re-dresses the wound on her husband's head.

SRENGI   Before I met you, this dagger was my only friend. I always offered it to anyone so that they could stab me with it.

SUANA   Get rid of it! Get rid of it!

SRENGI *(Her face is becoming angrier and angrier. She is becoming increasingly frightening.)* No one was able to fucking do it. I even went to the houses of the military and the nationalists and I offered them this dagger. But they just stared at it.

SUANA   Get rid of the fucking thing!

SRENGI   It turned out they weren't as vicious as the ones who dragged my husband away. Or those who made me do the Janger dance on top of his grave.

SUANA   Throw it AWAY!

Suddenly, it is as if everything stops. Srengi freezes. Her expression then slackens. Alit and the pair of Headless Ghosts disappear, as do Dura and Arini. The only sound is that of a crying baby, awoken from its sleep.

SRENGI   Let Dura get him up. I'm not able to. Dura is our only hope to win.

SUANA   He has already lost.

SRENGI   No. He cannot lose, not like us.

PART 12

Just like in the previous scene, in a corner of the house, Arini is treating Dura's wound and then applying some ointment to it. They're talking, but what they're talking about is unclear.

Suana and Srengi are sitting beneath the bed with their backs to each other.

SRENGI   That song... That dancing...

Srengi feels as though she will burst into tears. She fights against letting it out.

SUANA   Do you hate it?

SRENGI To hell with that song. But I like it... those sharp notes... And now our granddaughter is singing it. I don't want those melodies and that dance to become a part of her. I don't want Alit to experience such an accursed time. Me going through it is enough. The two of us is enough.

SUANA I saw you sing and dance to that song on stage during the Communist Party's campaign. You were a real star of the stage. A prima donna.

SRENGI I can't deny it. That song still flows through my veins. I can't get rid of it. I don't know why. Maybe because I don't want to. That song is both wild and beautiful.

SUANA You don't need to get rid of it. That song is the same as cockfighting. In the past, our ancestors held the cockfighting in the temples so that the spilt blood would be a kind of holy sacrifice. Now, it is just a kind of gambling. Cockfighting. It is a defeat.

There is silence.

The Janger song can be heard softly. It is sung beautifully. The song slowly becomes louder and louder. It is Srengi who is singing it! Alit appears and is performing the Janger dance, as if she is dancing to Srengi's singing. The two Headless Ghosts look on in amazement. The shadow of the excavator reappears. This time it is clearer.

PART 13

The excavator turns into a creature like a red bull, exhaling fiercely. It digs up the road, which has been marked with numbered poles. There is the hum of motors which is reminiscent of the sound of roads being built or houses being knocked down. Or the sound of a sword being dragged across rocks.

At the same time Arini is seen making an offering. She is making something out of coconut palm leaves with Srengi's dagger.

There is the sound of a politician making an inflammatory speech about the events in 1965, the 30th September Movement. From the sound of his words, it is clear that his speech comes from the trashy books that were published in the wake of the fall of the New Order government.

Then everything goes dark. All the sounds are swallowed up and the only sounds are those of a bell, chanting and prayers.

Dura and Arini appear in Balinese traditional clothes. Arini is carrying a basket of offerings. Dura takes a rooster from one of Suana's cages. They walk towards the little shrine at the bottom of the banyan tree. Arini makes the offering respectfully at the shrine. Dura takes something from behind his back. It is the small dagger belonging to his mother. He slits the throat of the rooster. Blood spills in front of the shrine.

The only sounds are those of the bell, chanting and prayers. Then, it is silent and dark.

The Janger song can be heard faintly. Alit sings it while sitting on the bed and holding tightly onto a hat. The hat that belonged to one of the Headless Ghosts.

Lights down.

The End.

Ibed Surgana Yuga

Ibed Surgana Yuga was born in Pancaseming, a village on the west side of Bali, Indonesia, 1983. He studied theatre direction at the Institute of the Arts of Yogyakarta (2003–2008). He is a playwright and director of Kalanari Theatre Movement, an organization through theatre based in Yogyakarta, which he founded in 2012. From 2005 till 2011, he worked as a playwright and director for Seni Teku, a theatre community which he founded in Yogyakarta. His collection of plays was published under the title *Kintir* (*Swept Away*) in 2011. Some of his plays have also been included in other Indonesian play anthologies.

His theatre works in Kalanari were mostly site-specific productions which traced stories and histories of the space where the performance was to be performed. Ibed is also a practitioner of body movement improvisation, for both arts and life purposes. In his hometown in Bali, he initiated Umah Solah, an open space for workshops and an arts laboratory. In 2011, he founded Kalabuku, a book publisher which specializes in publishing books on theatre and performance, and he works as an editor.

Red Janger (Indonesian title: *Janger Merah*) is one of his plays based on stories and histories of the massacre of those accused by the Indonesian Communist Party in 1965, in which his relatives were the victims.

Andy Fuller

Andy Fuller is an Australian researcher, translator and the author of *Sastra dan Politik: Membaca Karya-karya Seno Gumira Ajidarma* (Yogyakarta: Insist Press, 2011), *The Struggle for Soccer in Indonesia: Archives, Fandom and Urban Identity* (Yogyakarta: Tan Kinira, 2014) and *Playing Cities Making Sport* (Tan Kinira, 2014).

He is the translator of Afrizal Malna's poems as collected in *Anxiety Myths* (Lontar, 2014) and of A.S. Laksana's short stories (Lontar, 2015). He is also one of the editors of the *Lontar Anthology of Indonesian Short Stories* (Lontar, 2015).

He started Reading Sideways Press (RSP), a small press in Victoria, Australia, with Nuraini Juliastuti in 2018. RSP publishes books on the visual arts, literature and sports.

Playwright's Note:

Entering Indonesian history, I always felt like I was entering into a fairy tale. Because every storyteller has their own fantasy, and that makes me feel like I've never really known the truth.

So since 2015, I started to research on the theme 'history and fantasy' that I imagined in the form of a trilogy of plays, which I started, through an initial work called *Cut Off*.

I got an arts grant from the Kelola Foundation funded by HIVOS. I imagined the stories of Dutch colonialists, in which I created events that never existed in history. I imagined how slaves could fight and the melancholies of people who were colonized but then longed for the prosperous times of the colonial era.

In 2017, I continued my research by writing *Cut Out* as a second play in the trilogy, where I mixed the history of art and politics in Indonesia with questions about where modernism in Indonesia came from. However, instead of just repeating history, I included some of my own daily stories, both my very personal activities like someone who inhabits and becomes an active parasite of history, gnawing at it from within.

I will continue the final stage of my research, in this 'history and fantasy' trilogy by trying to trace the history of modern family construction in Indonesia, through the archives of modern realist drama scripts in Indonesia.

CUT OUT

Riyadhus Shalihin

Translated by Alfian Sa'at

A historical fiction constructed from various archival materials.

Characters

Can be performed by any number of performers, of any gender. The narration can be spoken by one actor or several.

Setting

A large screen which displays images of the numerous events depicted in the play. A bare stage in which various places are minimally suggested though props and costume.

FRAGMENT 1: A SUN WITH THE AROMA OF BURNT FLYING ANTS

NARRATION   The sound of birds chirping in the morning, a sign that today he is still alive, and just awoken. The voices of breakfast vendors, the vegetable seller who cries repeatedly: "Veggies, get your veggies" – walking with his two-wheeled cart cutting across from one street to another at the housing complex. Husbands and their wives, fathers and their children – revving the engines of their motorbikes and cars, in the yards of their houses – wives and their husbands, mothers and their children – ready with their bicycles to send their children to school, some gather in a corner shop, buying morning snacks, whether fried foods or cookies, to stave off hunger pangs. Today, in August, Bandung is not as chilly as usual, the dry season makes the morning feel warmer. He presses the number two button on a Miyako brand fan. A morning filled with the sounds of birds, vegetable vendors, motorised machines, conversations between fathers, mothers and children, and the hum of the electric fan: "nguuuuuung".

His ears seemed to possess an ability to focus on one thing at a time – and each thing they heard became visualized. Finches, sparrows, canaries, seagulls, pigeons, grouse, parrots, munias, figbirds, hummingbirds, crows, starlings were perched on their sleeping spots, on coffee cups, on hats, cabinets, clothes, brooms and mirrors. He was sitting in a large room – facing a tree that was standing tall, filled with several birds that were perching on the branches, jumping to and fro, as well as a Miyako fan with its humming and its whirl of dust. The birds seemed to have emerged from the bodies of other birds, each bird flapping its wings to move to another branch, and from within its wings other birds appeared, and so on.

The birds came closer and started to perch on his ears, nose, crown, the tips of his fingers and shoulders. The man stood up, heading for the tree in front of him, but with each step, his feet – slowly disappeared, as water foam bubbled to the surface, and the tree itself slowly sunk into the ground beneath his feet. A boat was sailing across the sea, as the birds lifted his body up – passing through Baghdad, Mecca, Medina and Jerusalem. The kingdom of Samudra Pasai in 1272, Arab and Persian Muslim traders – his soaking wet body is now down by the sea, along with his boat – he is trying to row towards the port when behind him a fish appears, still and calm, its eyes full of the memories of its journeys – through the thousands of ocean waves it has passed through – the sea leaving its traces in the salt smell of its body.

FISH I'm not dead. Life in this world is always moving. When the season comes round, we'll go home. Know yourself, trader. Make the ship ready for your return. Keep the rudder steady. So you can return soon. Fasten your riggings. Get in your supplies of water and wood. Place your oars over there. So that your boat will sail fast. The wood and water are on board. Now raise the anchors and the sails. Bring enough supplies of rice. The journey will surely be blessed and smooth.

NARRATION After uttering those words, the fish plunged to the bottom of the sea, and the splashing sound made by the fish's body woke the man up, who realized that he was still far from the edge of the city, so he rowed – but the more he rowed towards the shore, the more his boat drifted farther out to sea. By now the fish had become one with the ocean. On the right and left – dozens of boatmen seemed to be rushing in the direction of the city too, but the harder they rowed, the farther they were from the city, and a century passed, and they were still rowing. Then ships from the north arrived, hunting for spices, carrying black slaves, with cannons on their ships – explosions, unsheathed swords, banners, fluttering and flaming flags, boats arriving with telescopes, with priests singing hymns of salvation.

That evening, the sun set with a brilliant burst of light, insects from all corners of the island swarmed in the direction of the fading sun, burning themselves in union with the light. That afternoon the sun smelled of scorched insect wings, a sun with the aroma of burned flying ants.

FRAGMENT II: A COLONIAL FANTASY

NARRATION   He woke up again in his small room, in the city of Bandung – a room whose walls were covered in crayon scribbles. 12:00 am. There was the sound of seconds ticking away from the wall clock. All the residents of the building have fallen asleep, and occasionally there was the sound of wires clinking between the electricity poles — breaking the silence, before it became quiet again. He turned on his fan; it had been a baking hot night, sleep had deserted him, and his body was sweating a little. Turning to the Miyako fan, he pressed the number two button, until he could hear its blades whirring, rising in volume. It sounded like "nguuuuuuuuuuuuuuung". He sat down and looked at the fan. It was as if he was looking at a void, a void that had never been filled, deep and beyond reach. A void which kept the salty scent of the ocean. A void which contained the sound of war sirens, and thousands of ships coming from the north. 12:30 am. A chamber of the ship, VOC-schip De Amsterdam Batavialand.

The Miyako fan floated in the sky, then turned into lightning, into a storm. The ship rocked, and the Zeeland people cursed angrily in their own language. People with pinkish skin, and long noses, passed by the small porthole. Our man is neither here, nor is he there. Several people ran towards the ship's stern. A Governor-General of the Dutch East Indies, Johannes Van Den Bosch – was scratching a rash on his face, the cursed night and the ferocious mosquitoes of the Indies – made him uneasy. But the island he was heading towards was still far away. The sea was like a blanket wrapped around someone's body in the morning. He stood up tall – while holding the ship steady against the tossing waves.

JOHANNES VAN DEN BOSCH Don't ever forget that Javanese intellectuals do not develop beyond the capacity of our children who are 12 or 13 years old, and are actually more ignorant compared to those children. They must be led and governed like children.

NARRATION He heard the call to prayer, at 3:30 in the morning, but he still could not sleep. The call to prayer was everywhere, in the east, west and south of his city. Thirst raked his throat, he tried to reach for the glass under his bed, but his hand felt a puddle of water, then he tried to stand up, and realized that he was in the middle of the ocean, and that his bed was floating in the middle of the sea – with big ships all around him, with banners flapping on their hulls – they read: Gelderland, Zaandijk, Blijde Boodschap, Prinses Royaal. The man covered himself up with his blanket again. The cock crowed outside in the yard, he woke up, and it made him thirsty – so he reached out for the glass under his bed, but it disappeared as soon as it was touched by his hand, and so did the other objects, when he tried to touch a packet of Dji Sam Soe cigarettes, the mattress, a helmet, shoes, cabinets, a watch, hats, bags, carpets, prayer rugs, books, and clothes – they all disappeared. Good, now there was only his naked body and the Miyako fan. He always slept naked, and for him being naked in the room – it was like meeting his own self – his naked body had no intention of dressing up for any guests. "Nguuuuuuuuuung", there was only the sound of the fan. But now he was no longer feeling hot, instead, he was cold.

The sound of the fan slowly turned into the sound of dogs barking, growing louder by the minute. An empty room, the electric fan and the sound of dogs. A pack of dogs were barking while pulling at the leash of their handlers, checking every deck of the ship, lately it had been so easy to smuggle opium into Java. The Tanjung Perak Harbour, 1875. He was a member of a theatrical troupe, with costume trinkets and stage make-up, mirrors and powder. Someone who transformed into someone else, in another story, he not only inhabited that character – but also turned that character he played into an icon, into a past wrapped in parchment, before being sent to London, Paris and Leiden, into an Egyptian mummy of history watched by children on weekends. He was now in the company of a group of actresses and actors from three different troupes: Komedi Stamboel, Miss Riboet Orion and Opera Dardanella, now they were in the cosmopolitan city of Surabaya. The strains of the song *Surabaya Johnny* written by Bertolt Brecht and composed by Kurt Weill could be heard from loudspeakers at the edges of the harbour, excerpts of Carola Neher's singing from the musical opera *Happy End* at the Berlin Theater am Schiffbauerdamm (1929).

> *Du hast kein Herz, Johnny, Du bist ein Schuft, Johnny, Du gehst jetzt weg, Johnny, sag mir den Grund, Ich liebe dich doch, Johnny, Wie am ersten Tag, Johnny, Nimm die Pfeife aus dem Maul, du Hund. Surabaya-Johnny, warum bist du so roh? Surabaya-Johnny, mein Gott, ich liebe dich so. Surabaya-Johnny, warum bin ich nicht froh? Du hast kein Herz, Johnny, und ich liebe dich so.*

The man was naked, with stage costumes in his hands, in the middle of a crowd at the harbour. People were walking back and forth, slaves from Africa, traders from Siam, fishing boats at rest on the harbour's edge, the merchants, as well as travellers from the furthest reaches of the east and west. He was standing in the midst of chaos swirling around him, like a satellite tower – or a lighthouse. The lighthouse swung its beam to the east, to a pub – where there was a gathering of Auguste Mahieu (French), Tio Tik Djien (Chinese), Willy Klimanov (Russian), as well as Sayyed Aboe Bakar Bafaqih (Arab), they shared alcoholic drinks, reading highly anticipated drama scripts, before the end of the night their ship would sail to Batavia, they were wild and passionate, with high spirits – to welcome a native son who became a great painter in the land of Oranje, a painter who was no less skilful than Horace Vernet and Eugène Delacroix. This group of entertainers – on a full moon night, would move towards the Bataviasche Kunstkring, would open an exhibition commemorating Raden Saleh's return to Indonesia, with a performance of *Transnational Trading Company*, a play to welcome the arrival of new technology, as plantations in the Dutch East Indies began to fail.

The beam of light moved west, to an old castle in Dresden. AAJ Payen – a Belgian painter who worked for the Dutch, is teaching Raden Saleh to play the accordion, and written around the edges of an old timetable – a list of Raden Saleh's activities during his residency in the Netherlands, which include: attending a seminar on the "Character of the Nobility", a workshop on "The Architecture of tropical countries", "The Romantic movement in painting", all of which will be reported to De Lange (the Dutch financial inspector), who had brought Raden Saleh to the Netherlands. Meanwhile, some of the servants were busy stuffing piles of clothes into leather trunks. Raden Saleh would sail to the Dutch East Indies this week. The man then started wearing the clothes he was holding one by one, the costumes from the play *A Thousand and One Nights* which made him look like a Malay man trapped in the middle of the desert, the man then walked westwards – entering a cultural building, the Kolff Building, Jakarta. An exhibition guard told the man to dip his feet in a bucket of soap, the man remembered the smell of soap like the scent of burnt bubble gum, then the guard scrubbed the soles of his feet, and gave him a pair of Clarks shoes. The man entered the exhibition gallery, looking at pinkish-skinned, long-nosed people milling around – the gallery floor dotted with traces of soapy water from their feet. On the walls of the gallery, the man saw paintings from Maurice Utrillo, Paul Gauguin, Vincent Van Gogh, Odilon Redon, Raoul Dufy, Kees Van Dongen, Pablo Picasso, Vassily Kandinsky, Giorgio De Chirico, Massimo Campigli and Marc Chagall. Suddenly the song *Het Wilhelmus* was played - and the servants served wine – on the right side there stood Agus and Otto Djaja, Affandi Salim, and Mochtar Apin, who were being measured for their height and weight, on the right and left sides – large leather bags, a sign that very soon they would travel to distant places, where the trains and ships would belch out black smoke from burning coals, to London, Amsterdam, Brussels and Paris, cities where one cannot paint a truly blue sky, and thus in pursuit of the perfect light they travelled to the fields and the seas of the south of the Indies, to the rice fields and to the beach, hunting for the sublime glow of the afternoon – carefully painting shadows behind coconut trees and immortalizing them on postcards.

"TRAK!" The building lights went out, at 00:00 Western Indonesian Time, the man groped the walls of the building, looking for the light switch. The man sees a faint light at the end of the Kolff Building – he then goes towards the light, a vague sound from the future – echoing with an odd tempo and in an unfamiliar frequency:

> The Indonesian brain must be sharpened to match the Western brain! The individual must be animated with maximum life! The recognition of the importance of the self must reach maximum awareness! The nation of Indonesia must be encouraged to amass as much of the world's assets as possible; Indonesia must expand to all corners of the earth. Those who have assumed that all Easterners are virtuous saints while all Westerners are heartless villains will surely be surprised to hear that Eastern people must learn from the Westerners. This Spirit of Indonesia-ness that now revives our nation, which for centuries seemed like a dead man, we have in fact derived from the Western race.

FRAGMENT III: THE BURNING INDIES

NARRATION   His name was Bahroemsyah, just call him Bahroem, who was originally born in Langsa – his small hands were skilful, able to repair anything, from rice-polishers, to rice-weighing scales, to lorry dynamos, to train steam engines. Since 1920 – he has worked in the colonial service, graduating from HIS, 'Hollandsch-Inlandscheschool lit' / 'Dutch-Native School' / Primary School for Natives – schools for natives, specialising in mechanical engineering, which made him enrol in the field of railway engineering, then he was later transferred to become a road and bridge engineer, resulting in him touring the Dutch East Indies, to visit Siak, Kampar, Kelantan, Melaka, Tumasik, which were still mostly swampy forests, Formosa – Madagascar, to Tunisia. On that day, he was drafted as one of the crew members of the cruise ship "Exposition Coloniale Internationale" to Paris, France – in advance he had prepared himself, the best shoes, shirts and suits to withstand the weather at sea. His mother cooked beef rendang and chicken kalio, to eat during the trip, which would take two months, the act of stirring the rendang was precisely calculated – right and left, in one repetitive rotation of the clock, it was already the third day of Bahroem's mother boiling the rendang, watching the meat turn from red to blackish brown, and the white coconut milk to brownish yellow. A tantalizing fragrance– an aroma that would arouse the hunger of anyone who smelt it.

The man was still waiting for his other friends to come, theatre rehearsals always ended the same way – overrunning the specified schedule, the play *The Diamond Panner* by Kirdjomulyo that he would perform, a play that told the story of a man named Sanjoyo – who exiled himself to Kalimantan – because he felt inferior in front of his lover's wealthy parents, and his friend Siswadi went with him. A terrific play, emotionally draining, which made him unable to sleep – he would play the role of Siswadi – of course it would be challenging, it was the first time in his theatre career that he had a role with so much dialogue – since the afternoon he has been practising alone, in front of the gate, then moving to the roof of the building, then shouting while in the toilet, then in front of the park – then returning to the studio, and still no one was there – just himself and the stage set in the form of cut wood and planks. He sat down again – the studio was so quiet, especially on weekends like this, the man began to curse the stage manager who arbitrarily planned rehearsal schedules – who would want to rehearse for theatre, on a Sunday night? Then he cursed his own fate for not providing him with a partner. The studio was cold, with paint brushes and materials lying everywhere, used beer bottles, and a drumstick, used by the director to create tension during rehearsals, which almost hit his forehead, a theatre born from the director's confusions, a theatre of objects flung around by the management. He lit a Dji Sam Soe cigarette, the flame licking the cloves and tobacco, giving off a distinctive fragrance, the smoke he inhaled seeped into his lung's cavities – before finally being released, creeping along the ceiling of the building, and vanishing before managing to touch the roof. He heard the soft sound of the gamelan, the fragrance of frangipani flowers and incense filled the studio, the smoke slightly irritating the eyes of our male protagonist, drifting from the direction of the stage set – through the unfinished wooden door. Bahroem appeared with a sailor suit, walking purposefully, then other men appeared in the same suits, carrying large pieces of paper, they all emerged through the unfinished door on the set, carrying pliers, grinders, wooden beams, masks, tiles, bricks, iron boxes, krises, swords, spears and many other building tools and materials – they all hurried away, and vanished, swallowed up by the cloud of incense smoke.

BAHROEM   Siswadi – you're still not ready, this is your shirt. Hurry up and put it on. The ship's about to depart.

SISWADI   Do it.

NARRATION   That night millions of stars lit up the sky... Siswadi's body felt tired, he had just been transporting coal at the docks in Malaya. The ship would pass through the port of Andaman, then continue to the island of Ceylon, they would rest for a while in Madras, before raising anchor again. Siswadi then uttered a few words: *I have missed home for a long time already. I miss the city of Bandung, where I grew up.*

A forest on the outskirts of Paris, July 1931. Across Lake Daumesnil. The Vincennes Maillot line is expanded to service the exhibition site, two new stations: Porte Dorée and Porte de Charenton, are built. Carpenters from Belgium, Denmark, the Netherlands and Portugal are seen bustling to and fro – Italy, which controlled Tripolitana, Eritrea and Somalia – was building an ancient Roman basilica. France was busy promoting "La Grande France" by reconstructing the temple of Angkor Wat in Paris, including a relief of the Ramayana stretching for 1 kilometre, that eventually became the symbol of the "Expo". Bahroem and Siswadi – were still laying bricks in order to complete the Dutch East Indies' pavilion, with only one month before the pavilion was due to be opened, and opposite the construction – Moojen was sleeping on his side, while beside him Zweedik was opening the paper tube containing the building plans. Bahroem lifted up a few pieces of wood – and put them down again. Siswadi pushed the wheelbarrow, filled with wood, through the temple-style gate. Wood was being used to cut the costs of the building, this eleven thousand square metre building called the East Indies would arouse pride in the Dutch, in front of Britain and France. Siswadi wiped his sweat with his shirt.

BAHROEM   You don't usually work hard, do you?

SISWADI I used to pan for diamonds in the river. At the Gula River – Central Kalimantan, accompanying my friend – his name's Sanjoyo, from Yogyakarta. I'm indebted to him, he was tortured by the Dutch colonial police for keeping my whereabouts a secret.

BAHROEM Was life better there?

SISWADI Not really, sometimes there were landslides.

MOOJEN *Vrij snel, we zijn tijd nodig.*

BAHROEM *Ja, Meneer.*

NARRATION Siswadi looked at the street, so many people had gathered, packing it right to the edge of the forest, they carried posters and banners that read: *"Rejette expo coloniale", "Civilization Vampires", "Nous sommes contre une exposition inhumaine"*, dressed in suits, and pantaloons, they sat around, lighting pipes, smoking. As time wore on, the gathering became increasingly bigger, and more crowded.

BAHROEM They call themselves the "Surrealists".

NARRATION Siswadi did not understand Bahroem's answer. Siswadi was only paying attention to the rhythm of hammering plank after plank of wood, which then slowly built up, forming a pitched roof. Lumps of wood seemed as if they were growing their own hands, they were alive – arranging themselves, shoulder to shoulder, to form a roof on this monument. Siswadi was stunned to see the choreography of the wood: he felt himself disappear and started muttering again, excerpts of the dialogue from the drama *The Diamond Panner*: *"We better hurry home, Sanjoyo. We've been wandering a long time."* Then he noticed fire crawling up the sides of the building, creeping like a snake, licking whatever it passed, demolishing wooden doors with Jepara carvings, devouring collections of batik cloth from Bali and Flores stored in display boxes, krises and swords, scabbards of gold and silver, ivory and wood. Precious stones, ancient statues – symbols of the Gods from the primitive Hindu era, ancient and antique musical instruments. The smell of incense spread. Balinese dancers ran out half-naked, gripped by panic. The smell of burnt wood and charcoal. Siswadi felt he had returned home, transported by mantras and music, prayers from the dancers, casting out evil spirits. The building was totally blackened. Springtime was dotted with embers. The burning Beautiful Indies turned into black smoke in the European sky. Audience applause could be heard, in the theatre building – but he was no longer Siswadi – he was the rubble from the bonfire of colonialism, his costume stained with the blood spilled by beauty.

FRAGMENT IV: DAD HAS NEVER RETURNED

NARRATION   A hotel room at 'Tokyu Stay' – Ikebukuro – Toshima City, Tokyo, November 1988. Nadya felt that she had not really arrived at her present location, the shadow of her missing father was still haunting her. After the year 1943 – Nadya's father was suspected of involvement in the Japanese anti-fascist movement, several times the Kempeitai secret police arrested him with Amir Sjarifoeddin, Nadya was only 2 years old at the time. Now nearing the age of 45 – Nadya never really forgot how her father had run away from home, without her having the chance to really memorize the look on his face, she could only recall the fragrance of his hair oil, her nose always seemed to pick up her father's presence, insisting to her that he had not really disappeared. The veins in her hands were becoming increasingly visible – her hands turned the hot water lever for the shower, the water sprayed on Nadya's head, creating a massaging sensation, slowly erasing the cold from her skin, a skin that was filled with longing, layers of skin that that were full of questions.

NADYA   Did someone say he was in Singapore, Ma?

MOTHER   But that was ten years ago. Wak Giman smuggled him to Singapore, and Taiwan. But later there was no news about your father.

NADYA   What did father really look like, Ma?

NARRATION   Nadya was sometimes bored, during that year – the news was always delivered with the same headlines. Nadya would often ask, were there no sentences that were more creative, that would inspire one's intellectual curiosity, or was everything just entertainment?

RADIO YEAR 1944 *Achieving the final victory in the holy* war. *Join to become a Romusha volunteer. I am willing to work to find friends to become Romusha volunteers to be sent to the relief organization for work soldiers.*

NARRATION   On March 8, 1942, in Kalijati, Lieutenant General Ter Poorten (the Netherlands) surrendered to Japan, and on March 27, 1942, the Dai Nippon Army pledged laws promising welfare and protection for Indonesia. The cultural organization Keimin Bunka Shidoso was established, the triple A espionage organisation was formed, rhetorical speeches were made about the future of Greater East Asia. Nadya felt that she did not want to be a part of history, any history, a history that could not bring a human being back from oblivion. The window of her hotel room was fogged up, Nadya looked at the street outside her hotel, young girls with their partners, young men in neat suits and their luxurious cars. Nadya still hoped that among the saké inns, or the Family Mart which was open 24 hours, there was someone waiting for her – someone she might share a coffee with. This was the 8th year of her search, and she would spend the next two weeks with a divided spirit, between Indonesia and Japan, between Yogyakarta and Tokyo – she would miss her mother's *Mangut Lele* or Aunt Mun's *Chicken Kalio*. Her mother was a champion cook with simple spices – fresh Javanese ones – and her aunt – an expert at processing coconut milk into all kinds of rich, spicy food. There were no *kemangi* leaves in Tokyo, or *Balado Terong*. Tokyo – it might have never revealed to her where her father was, but by being here, she knew where he was, in this land – a land whose soldiers had made her father disappear, it was as if she was binding herself within a strange circle of melancholy.

BAHROEM   Where is your husband?
MOTHER   Where is your father?
NADYA   I did not see him. His skullcap and clothes were the only things I found...

FRAGMENT V: RAIN AT PRENZLAUER BERG

NARRATION The edges of the trees could be seen from the window, as if marking the boundary between the roof of the house and the veranda of the apartment. A cloudy afternoon in the Senefelderstrasse area of Berlin, after a short walk – after 2 pm he would pass through the park in the Lilli-Henoch-Strasse area, where he would sit around the statue of the face of Ernst Thalmann, leader of the Weimar republic, a resolute statue typical of Soviet realism, designed by Lev Kerbel. It was early summer, May, with cold winds still blowing, but nevertheless one could sense the joy as people welcomed the fresh air – Gigok remembered the week before, on the 1st of May – together with his next-door neighbour at the apartment – Claudia Brauer, walking together to the Kreuzberg area. The cramped U-Bahn in East Berlin was getting increasingly crowded with young people, sipping alcohol – passing through the crowd at Görlitzer Bahnhof, participating in the May Day World Labour Day celebration. A worldwide holiday for workers, which felt more like a cultural festival. In the midst of the hustle and bustle – Gigok would sit alone and remember Nadya, his daughter.

CLAUDIA BRAUER *Erinnerst du dich nochmal?*

GIGOK *Ah nein, es hat nur einen Moment gekreuzt?*

NARRATION Wak Giman's face – he could not recall it as clearly anymore. Age had attacked his memory like termites, until there was nothing left but brittle fragments, dust from the past. Claudia Brauer had invited him for a stroll, of course Gigok would always be interested. There was nothing more enjoyable than walking, every footstep claiming space for itself, absorbing the scent of the streets, telling the streets of Berlin – that someone called Gigok was still alive, was still there and breathing. Now here he was again – in the Dorotheenstadt Cemetery, Berlin, Chausseestrasse – next to the house of Bertolt Brecht, a cemetery for many artists and thinkers – those who came from East Germany were buried here, but Gigok was only an expert in repairing clocks – he often wondered, was there also someone who repaired clocks laid to rest there? Gigok often asked, was it possible that a Communist who came from a country that did not yet exist – could come to be buried there, in the same place as Heiner Müller, even the headstone of Heiner Müller looked diffident, with a name carved into a tall brown stone, slender and small – almost submerged unseen, by the overgrown bushes, and their masking shadows – a tombstone that was hard to find, maybe Gigok's headstone would just be a mound of red earth. Gigok never got to know his country, which later became liberated from Japan, Gigok escaped when it was known as the Dutch East Indies – two years before his homeland became independent – Singapore, Taiwan, Islamabad, Bhutan, Saigon – he remembered the names of the cities he had wandered through, destitute, but he had almost forgotten the smell of Yogyakarta city.

Madiun 1948, Musso died, Amir Sjarifudin was captured, and died in Surakarta. The migration of the central government of the Republic of Indonesia to Yogyakarta (1946-1949). The failed Communist uprising from 1926 to 1927, the Indonesian Communist Party was declared a banned party. November 1965 – D.N. Aidit was killed in Boyolali. Hundreds of thousands of Communist sympathizers throughout Indonesia were hunted down and massacred. The Indonesian Communist Party, which was the third largest communist party in the world – was destroyed and disappeared. Rain began to fall. Rain with a thousand sorrows from children who had lost their fathers, lost their mothers, children who kept on being transferred from cell to cell. Gigok just wanted to hug Nadya, to kiss her forehead – while singing a birthday song. Gigok wanted to walk as someone without history, in front of Bernauer Strasse, he wanted to be one of the iron pillars rusted by age – or to become the ruins of houses that were torn down to form Berlin's city boundaries, to become the crumbs of pigeon food at Karl-Liebknecht-Strasse – in front of the statue of a seated Karl Marx – in front of dozens of eyes belonging to people sitting in the park – who could not give him back the memories of growing up with a child: the faint strains of music:

Arise the wretched of the earth, arise prisoners of starvation.

So comrades, come rally

and the last fight let us face.

The Internationale unites the human race.

FRAGMENT VI: SOMEONE WHO IS INHABITING ANOTHER'S STORY

NARRATION   At Suminta's house in Jakarta, or more precisely: in a small central room, which was filled with battered furniture – one morning the atmosphere was gloomy and lonely, as if not a soul had lived there. Our male hero – is brewing coffee, watching Mini walk to and fro, putting on makeup and getting ready to leave the house. Suminta was silent – staring blankly.

OUR MAN   Don't be too hard on yourself, being faithful to me doesn't mean having no fun.

MINI   I'm going now.

OUR MAN   Don't go yet, because on the next page you'll be seduced by a man in a car, because you'll need money to buy cooking oil and fried noodles, and one of your neighbours will see you and report it to your husband, of course your husband will get angry, then you'll fight, and your husband will choose to leave this house – to leave you all by yourself, so let's discuss this family's financial problems first, then you may go out, and that's assuming that you will.

NARRATION   The interior of an old house, run down and neglected. An old set of chairs, an old metal bed. A room that gave the impression of it being a space for death. A flower vase with dried and dead plants. Bright lighting. Quiet. Nadya – began to slowly paint the room, turning it white, the tables were painted white, the old metal bed was painted white – the room's windows were opened, the morning air entered the room – replacing the dried plants with fresh roses – turning on the theatre stage lights until everything was visible and exposed. Wijasti was face to face with a man named Karnowo who was about to rape her; Karnowo had a grudge against her father – who had destroyed his lover.

WIJASTI   You'll really take it. That thing that is valuable only once in a woman's life.

NADYA   Karnowo – listen to me, Wijasti is not the biological child of Kardiman, because Kardiman married Wijasti's mother who was already pregnant – by her boyfriend before marriage. So, there's no point – put on your shirt and pants again, then pick up your friend Kardiman, and let's have some tea.

NARRATION   Suminta made tea for all the stories in this room, tea for Kardiman, Karnowo, Wijasti, Mini, Our Man, Gigok, Wak Giman, Claudia, Mother and Nadya – all of them gathered in the living room in the house. A sofa, a table and a television set. Photos of a father, mother and child. A painting of the Kaaba (Mecca) on the wall. Nadya turned the television on to TVRI – 1978, for the third time Suharto was re-elected as president, the announcement of the General Assembly of the MPR and the Inauguration of the President and Vice President of the Republic of Indonesia. The Indonesian Armed Forces entered the villages, transmigration from overcrowded Java to less crowded Sumatra. Advertisements extolling that "Two Children Are Enough". Norms promoted of Small Families which were happy and prosperous.

With family planning we will have a healthy, prosperous family, physically, spiritually and socially. It is time for family planning, have no doubt about it. Family planning is very meaningful. For a glorious future, and healthy children. Smart and strong, the hope of the nation. Come on, happy mothers, for the prosperity and harmony of your households.

The city of Jakarta with the completed MRT line. Jabodetabek KRL-Commuterline, a carriage "Exclusively Reserved for Women". In pink and decorated with roses. At 17:30, the route home from work. All passengers are holding their own smart devices. The slow and distant coming and going of airplanes, the hum of ultrasonic sounds, the CCTV footage of a quiet corner of a public bathroom, the noisy recordings of wiretaps in the State Palace. There is no one at the dining table, there is nobody to turn off the television that is still broadcasting, nobody comes, and nobody leaves.

Lights down.

The End.

Archive Reference List

Fragment I – From the poetry collection *Poem of the Boat* by Hamzah Fansuri (1590).

Fragment III – From the play *The Diamond Panner* by Kirdjomulyo

Fragment IV – From the play *Father's Home* by Usmar Ismail (1942)

Fragment VI – From the drama script *Unfortunately There's Someone Else* by Utuy Tatang Sontani (1955) and *Dusk and Two Deaths* by Kirdjomulyo (1966)

Riyadhus Shalihin

Riyadhus is a young dramaturg, playwright and theatre director who has taken part in the International Forum Theatertreffen, Berlin, Germany (2019), Art Camp Asian Performing Arts Forum, Tokyo, Japan (2018), Curators' Academy Theaterworks, Singapore (2018), Asean Theatre – Central Cultural Centre Philippines, Manila (2013).

In 2018, his video artwork *Unidentified Origin of the Lightless* won first prize in the Ritz Carlton Bazaar Video Art, Jakarta, and his play *Cut Out* was selected as the winner of the Rawayan Award (playwright forum) and became the title of the book (2018). In 2019, his play *Cut Out* was performed at Ovalhouse Theatre, London directed by Kumiko Mendl in a showcase of Indonesian Plays, organized by Indonesia Dramatic Reading Festival.

He is a founding member and artistic director of Bandung Performing Arts Forum (B.P.A.F.) which includes directing an international collaboration project with Theatre MUIBO from Tokyo in *The Fallen Boat,* Bandung, 2019 – with Leow Puay Tin from Malaysia in *Us Not Us* in Asian Dramaturg Network, Yogyakarta, 2018. He also worked as a dramaturg on *Holy-Body* for Salihara International Dance Festival HELATARI, Jakarta 2019. For him, archives offer a range of perspectives. He often plays around with archives, rearranging the historical events, and celebrating them as a form of social imagination, not as frozen material in museums, or static silent text in libraries.

Alfian Sa'at

Alfian is a Resident Playwright with W!LD RICE, one of Singapore's most recognized theatre companies. His published works include three collections of poetry, *One Fierce Hour, A History of Amnesia, The Invisible Manuscript*, a collection of short stories, *Corridor*, a collection of flash fiction, *Malay Sketches*, three collections of plays, as well as the published play *Cooling Off Day*.

He has been nominated eleven times for Best Original Script at the Life! Theatre Awards, eventually winning in 2005 for *Landmarks*, in 2010 for *Nadirah*, in 2013 for *Kakak Kau Punya Laki (Your Sister's Husband)* and in 2016 for *Hotel* (with Marcia Vanderstraaten).

In 2011, he was awarded the Boh-Cameronian Award in Malaysia for Best Book and Lyrics for the musical *The Secret Life of Nora*. In 2013, he won the Boh-Cameronian Award for Best Original Script for the play *Parah*. In 2001, he won the Golden Point Award for Poetry as well as the National Arts Council Young Artist Award for Literature. He has also been nominated for the Singapore Literature Prize three times, for *Corridor* (Commendation Prize, 1999), *A History of Amnesia* (2004) and his translation of the novel *The Widower* (2016).

SIN

TRISA TRIANDESA

based on the novel *Not a Virgin* by Nuril Basri

edited and translated by John H. McGlynn

Characters

RICKY A good-looking but poor vocational highschool student living in a *pesantren*; 18 years of age and of uncertain sexual orientation.

PARIS A wealthy vocational highschool student and a classmate of Ricky who wants to be a woman.

YUSUF Ricky's roommate at the *pesantren,* an orphan from childhood who was raised at the *pesantren*. He is somewhat effeminate, and though one year younger than Ricky, he is already aware of his sexual preference.

Settings

A *pesantren* where Ricky and Yusuf live.

A gay club in Jakarta where the three characters begin to discover their identities.

A hotel room or hotel rooms.

Time The present.

INT. PESANTREN. DAY

Ricky enters wearing a sarong and a long-sleeve, collarless and blousy white shirt, with a white peci on his head. In the crook of his right arm is a prayer rug. In his right hand he holds the Quran and a kitab kuning or "yellow book," which he has been trying with difficulty to read.

RICKY *(to the audience)* Not everyone who lives in in this *pesantren* is here to study religion. Some of the guys ran away from home and had nowhere else to go; some were kicked out of their homes; and then there are others whose lives are so directionless that the *pesantren* was the easiest choice for them. *(paces back and forth on the left side of the stage)* At any rate, I never thought I'd have to live in a *pesantren*, but here I am. And it's not because I wanted to learn how to read the Quran. That I can do — even if I don't know what the words mean. I'm here because my brother got married and he and his wife took over my room.

Since coming here, I've been living two lives: a religious life here at the *pesantren* and that of a regular vocational highschool student outside.

But my life is far from normal any more.

Not since meeting Paris, anyway....

Paris.... No, don't picture Paris Hilton. This Paris's real name is "Muhammad Farisy." Funny though, that he's Christian with a name like that.

And what is Paris to me? Even though we are the same age, Paris is — What's the word? — my "benefactor". The long and short of it is that, for some reason, Paris took a shine to me and, dirt poor that I am, I've let him play that role — which, I guess, makes me his kept boy.

Ricky exits.

INT. PESANTREN. DAY

From offstage, the sound of a car is heard. The car engine grows louder then dies. A car door is opened then closed. Paris enters dressed in highschool uniform with a tote bag in one hand and car keys in the other. Ricky, now dressed in a highschool uniform as well, follows behind.

PARIS You should have come to the salon with me. *(tries to straighten Ricky's hair with his fingers)* You need to do something with your hair.

RICKY *(shrugging Paris aside)* Don't touch me like that. Somebody might see. You can act like a queen outside but not here!

PARIS Oh, please, don't tell me there aren't any other queens here.

Ricky and Paris go into Ricky's bedroom where Yusuf is seated, ladylike, atop his mattress on the floor. The room is a simple one with just one rickety looking armoire and two thin mattresses on a mat-covered floor.

PARIS *(eyeing Yusuf and then Ricky)* See what I said!

Ricky elbows Paris.

RICKY Paris, meet Yusuf, my cellmate. *(Paris looks at him, confused.)* "Cell" is the term we use for rooms at the *pesantren* here. *(To Yusuf)* Shouldn't you be at recitation lessons?

YUSUF Booooring!

PARIS *(looking around and making a face)* This is your bedroom? Looks more like a shed to me.

RICKY Don't be so snooty. We have homework to do. *(To Yusuf)* Move aside; we're here to do our homework.

Ricky and Paris remove tools and assignment books from their bags.

PARIS I hate this kind of thing.

RICKY What kind of thing?

PARIS You know: this homework — all these mechanical lessons with hydraulic systems, jacks, oil pumps, disc brakes, whatever. I'd do better with knitting needles than this kind of thing.

RICKY Well, why are you in vocational high school if you don't like it?

PARIS My papa forced me...

RICKY Your father forced you?

PARIS He said it would make me a man.

Beat.

Paris takes out an iPhone X from his bag, which draws Yusuf's attention.

YUSUF Wow! You have iPhone X? Do you have internet?

PARIS *(to Yusuf)* Of course. *(To Ricky)* By the way, what's your Instagram?

RICKY Not my kind of thing.

PARIS Facebook?

Ricky shrugs.

RICKY I'm going to take a bath. *(takes a towel and exits)*

PARIS *(offhandedly to Yusuf)* Do you want to use the internet?

YUSUF *(enthusiastically)* Will you teach me? I want to be on Facebook and Instagram so that I can meet new people outside this place.

PARIS "Meet new people", huh? I see... You mean like a dating app?

YUSUF Yes!

PARIS Well, do you like guys or girls?

YUSUF What kind of question is that?!

PARIS Oh sorry...

YUSUF Guys, of course!

PARIS Well first, you need an email account...

Paris quickly creates an email account for Yusuf, then takes a picture of him.

PARIS Now, let's go to Grindr... Um, what do you want your profile name to be?

YUSUF "Desperate"!

Again very quickly Paris creates a Grindr account for Yusuf then starts to teach Yusuf how to use it. On an onstage screen a page appears with multiple obscene profile photos. Ricky enters the room to see Yusuf sending messages to profiles of various older men. Ricky shuts his eyes and shakes his head.

RICKY *(to Paris)* What are you teaching him? How to chat with men? Look at that — those naked pictures!

PARIS Hey, I'm just trying to broaden his horizons. And what's wrong chatting with men?

RICKY *(whispering to Paris)* But what if he turns gay?

PARIS *(staring at Ricky in disbelief)* Duh...

Yusuf stands and returns the smartphone to Paris.

YUSUF Thanks, Paris, but I have to go now. I have work to do.

RICKY Since when did you get a job?

YUSUF Just today, in fact. I met this guy at the mall who said he needed some help with sales. *(exits)*

Blackout.

INT. PESANTREN. EARLY MORNING

It's early morning and Ricky is asleep in his room. Yusuf tiptoes quietly into the room but causes Ricky to wake.

RICKY Hey, where were you?

YUSUF *(startled)* Shit, you scared me!

Yusuf sits down on his mattress and takes out a small packet wrapped in white paper.

RICKY What's that?

YUSUF *(with his index finger to his lips)* Shhh... It's shabu.

RICKY Japanese food?

YUSUF No. Meth, you dummy.

RICKY Are you crazy?! You can't use that here!

YUSUF I'm not using it; I'm selling it, moron!

RICKY So that's your sales work? *(Yusuf nods.)* You could get thrown in jail, you know.

YUSUF *(fluttering his hand dismissively)* Not gonna happen. The guy I got it from says he has police backing. *(Beat)* Well, don't just lie there. Help me to pack this stuff!

RICKY No way.

YUSUF *(coyly)* Please, pretty please. Help me.

Yusuf keeps pulling on Ricky's blanket until he finally sits up and starts to help Yusuf to divide up the cake of shabu and put it into small plastic bags.

RICKY But who are you going to sell it to?

YUSUF Oh, to the other boarders — or maybe to the teacher! *(giggling)* Wouldn't that be a kick, to fly as we learn to recite!

RICKY Lunatic…

YUSUF Come on… As if you don't know that there are lots of guys here who aren't treading the holy path. *(Ricky stares at him until Yusuf sighs.)* Don't worry, I'm not selling it here. There are plenty of rich kids at the mall looking for the stuff.

RICKY So, if you sell this stuff, what are you going to buy?

YUSUF First, a nice prayer sarong, and then… my own smart phone!

Blackout.

INT. PESANTREN. LATE AFTERNOON

Ricky and Paris, dressed in school uniforms, enter Ricky's cell to find Yusuf busily chatting on a new cellphone.

YUSUF *(shouting happily to Paris)* Look at what I got!

PARIS Ooh fancy! When did you get that?

YUSUF *(continuing to chat as he replies)* Just yesterday. *(breathlessly)* And that's not all I got!

RICKY What else did you get? A prayer sarong?

YUSUF *(to Paris)* I also got a daddy!

RICKY What's a daddy?

PARIS *(looking at the cellphone screen)* Is that him? Oh my!

RICKY Yuck! Why do you want to meet old men?

YUSUF *(setting aside his cellphone and speaking in an imploring voice)* Will you go clubbing with me? My daddy here gave me the name of a club and asked me to meet him there this coming Saturday.

RICKY A club? What kind of club? You can't go clubbing?

YUSUF Why not?

RICKY You're a religious student.

YUSUF Well, so what?

PARIS *(peremptorily)* Okay! Saturday night we'll go clubbing! *(To Ricky)* You, too, Ricky. And it's about time we brought you into the modern world. *(removing a cellphone from his bag)* Here, this is my old phone. Now learn how to use it so that I can contact you more. *(Beat.)*

Ricky appears shocked and confused.

Blackout.

EXT. STARLIGHT. NIGHT.

Ricky, Paris, Yusuf arrive at Starlight, a gay club in a dodgy building that looks more like a warehouse than a club. The sound of house music from inside the bar can be heard.

RICKY *(hesitant)* What are we doing here? I've never been to a bar before.

PARIS Stop worrying. It will be fun! Nobody knows us and nobody cares who we are.

RICKY You just want to get drunk and forget who you are.

PARIS No, Ricky, I don't want to get drunk. I just want to watch other people. Is that such a sin?

RICKY But what kind of place is this? It's almost all guys.

PARIS *(incredulous)* You don't know what this place is…? It's a place for the likes of Yusuf — and maybe you, too.

Dance music grows louder. Ricky still looks uncomfortable. Yusuf seems excited and begins to move with the melody.

YUSUF Come on, let's go in!

As Yusuf opens the door, the sound of an announcement is heard. The bar's weekly drag show is about to begin. People in the club whistle and applaud.

RICKY Oh, well, I gotta piss anyway…

Blackout.

EXT. PESANTREN. DAY

Ricky is dressed in a loose, black martial arts outfit and is practising pencak silat moves. Now, much more than when dressed in his school uniform, he appears athletic, with a well-proportioned body.

RICKY For the past couple months I've been taking *pencak silat* lessons with Ustaz Asman, the new recitation teacher here.

I like this physical stuff but not all the recitation business. That makes me want to throw up.

Ustaz Asman said he could also teach me *kebatinan*. He said muscles aren't always enough to protect oneself, that I should try to acquire this mental or spiritual power too. But the requirements are crazy!

First, there's a white fast where you can't eat anything that's not white for forty days — like rice, cassava and water — and you're supposed to wear all white clothing, too.

On top of that, every night, you have to recite a special prayer for a thousand times without a break. If you pause or stumble, you have to start over.

I asked him if there was an easier way, and he said that it was possible but very expensive. He wouldn't say how much exactly but when I started counting upwards he didn't stop shaking his head until I'd reached the figure of fifteen million rupiah.

Fifteen million rupiah...! Amazing, I thought, supernatural powers for sale!

Even then, there was still another catch. I have just forty days to get that amount.

On the onstage screen, a visual of Ricky's cellphone screen appears. It's a text message from Paris: "We're going to a hotel!"

RICKY *(muttering to himself)* Hotel? *(To the audience)* So, I guess the time has come for me to finally put out. I shouldn't be surprised, I guess. Paris has been paying all my expenses for months now. But, truthfully, I never thought it would come to this. I never thought I'd lose my virginity this way.

INT. HOTEL. DAY

In the hotel room, Ricky is sitting nervously on the end of the bed while Paris is in the bathroom, speaking to him from behind the partially closed door.

PARIS Rick... Ricky...?

RICKY Yeah?

PARIS Are you sure you're ready for this?

RICKY *(in a resigned voice)* Yeah, I'm ready...

PARIS I've always wanted to do this but, but...

RICKY But what?

PARIS I've never had the guts. It's only you, Ricky, only you I feel comfortable enough with, I swear... I hope you won't hate me afterwards. I just want to be myself for once... Are you ready, Ricky?

Ricky rises and begins to take off his clothes, stripping down to just his underwear. While doing this, he speaks to the audience.

RICKY   Geez, what's with all the melodrama? I'm not happy here. I just want to do it and get it over with. Whether I hate him afterwards is my business, something for me to deal with.

PARIS   Rick, you don't know how hard it was for me to come to this decision... Are you ready?

RICKY   I'm ready.

PARIS   Are you really?

RICKY   Yes, I really am.

PARIS   But are you really?

The sound of the bathroom door as it is slowly opened and Paris emerges dressed in women's clothing: a tight blouse and skirt with an oversize snakeskin belt and black stockings. A cheap wig covers his head; a thick layer of powder covers his face. He has heavily made-up eyes and lashes plus flaming red lipstick. Ricky is shocked by the sight of him, but Paris is equally flummoxed to see Ricky only in his underwear.

PARIS & RICKY *(simultaneously)* What the...?!

PARIS *(puzzled)* What are you doing without your clothes?

RICKY *(even more puzzled)* Well, what are you doing in those clothes. You want to pretend to be a woman when we do it?

PARIS   When we do what?

RICKY   You know, screw, or whatever two guys do. That's why you asked me here, isn't it?

PARIS   Are you out of your mind? I don't want to do anything with you!

RICKY   Well then, what are we doing here?

PARIS   I wanted you to see me, is all. To tell me if I'm pretty or not! I just want to know what you think, not to screw. Don't you get it, Ricky? I want to be a woman!

RICKY   Even if you dress in women's clothing, you're still a guy. That's just the way you were born.

PARIS But I'm really a woman inside! Is that so hard for you to understand!

Paris breaks into tears and slumps to the floor. Ricky falls to his knees and takes Paris into his arms.

Blackout.

INT. STARLIGHT. NIGHT

Ricky is seated in a corner of the bar looking uncomfortable. From the direction of the changing room, Yusuf approaches, dressed in women's clothing.

RICKY *(looking Yusuf up and down)* What the hell...! Why are you dressed like that?

YUSUF Because I need to practise! Every week there's a drag show here, and next week is the start of Starlight's Miss Drag Queen contest. But tonight *(handing a flyer to Ricky)* — which is why I brought you here! — it's an Angel Boy contest! It will be fun and the money's not bad if you win. You need the money, don't you?

RICKY How much?

YUSUF A million, I think. Plus, if you win, the boss here will pay you to work the floor and you can keep all the tips!

RICKY *(to the audience)* That would go a ways towards paying Ustaz Asman. Paris won't help me with that. *(To Yusuf)* But what do I have to do? Not screw the judges, I hope?

YUSUF *(laughing)* That's my department. Leave those old men to me! *(dragging Ricky to the side of the stage)* All you got to do is walk up and down the catwalk... In your underwear.

Yusuf pulls off Ricky's clothes, leaving him wearing nothing but an old pair of underpants.

YUSUF All you have to do is walk. No need to panic.

Ricky's name is called. Yusuf pushes Ricky on to the catwalk.

A brief pause.

MC　　　　　　And here he is: Ricky! Starlight's newest angel!

As winner of the contest, a pair of angel wings is attached to Ricky's back.

Blackout.

EXT. PESANTREN. DAY

Ricky is practising pencak silat moves and is now in even better shape than before. As he makes his moves, he speaks to the audience.

RICKY　　　　After becoming an Angel Boy, it didn't take me long to get into the swing of things and I was working at Starlight a few nights a week.

The tips were good and, to be truthful, I liked the attention — which was something I never had in my life before. I joined a gym and started working out regularly, but not just for that...

The men I met there would often invite me to dinner and buy me things. They'd give me money, too.

All I had to do was spend time with them. I got new clothes; a new cellphone too, and like Yusuf, soon discovered a new source of income from the guys I met online.

Amazing how many lonely old guys there are in the world, men who only need another man to be with them and to listen to them.

Busy as I was, I wasn't able to spend much time with Paris. I missed our time together, but I noticed that he, too, was changing—becoming more confident and more comfortable with himself.

And Yusuf? He was getting more aggressive — and more outlandish — all the time.

INT. STARLIGHT. NIGHT

Ricky is standing near the bar, dressed only in his underwear but this time it is brand-name underwear and he now looks much more professional. Paris enters dressed in casual women's attire: loose slacks, white blouse and low heels. His long hair looks silken in the light.

RICKY *(looking at Paris)* Hey, you look nice. *(under his breath)* A lot better than the first time! *(to Paris)* What's up?

PARIS I was just in the Ladies' room. I was talking to Dolly — you know, the photographer who comes here — and she said that she'd like to hire you for a night. She said it would be worth your time. Ten million, just for one night!

RICKY Did she say what I have to do?

PARIS That amount of money, I'd guess she wants to take nude photographs of you but maybe, maybe it's something else... *(as if inspired)* Like a raffle party for rich wives where you are the prize! *(laughing)*

RICKY What are you talking about?

PARIS You must have heard about such parties before — get-togethers for bored rich housewives whose husbands don't satisfy them where the lucky draw is not Tupperware but a hunky young man like you.

RICKY I don't believe you.

PARIS Well don't then, but for ten million, there must be sex involved.

RICKY Well, I'd sure like the money but having sex with an old woman. Shit, I've never even done it before. I'm not like Yusuf, you know.

Yusuf suddenly appears in spectacular-looking clothes, Ariana Grande-ish.

YUSUF Someone mention my name?

PARIS Ricky was just saying that you're not a virgin.

YUSUF *(with hand to forehead)* It's true! I lost my virginity at a five-star hotel — or was it seven? I can't remember — with five old Arab guys, all at once. Sheiks they were. And I had to service everyone! I felt just like Maria Ozawa. And the next morning, my body felt crushed but, ohmygod, I felt so sexy...

Both Ricky and Paris make a face.

PARIS That's disgusting.

YUSUF *(wistfully)* Of course, I'd once dreamed of surrendering my virginity to a man I loved... Of making love beneath a full moon or, oh my God, something romantic like that...

PARIS You little sinner, you!

YUSUF Who's talking? You're no virgin either.

PARIS Excuse me! I am so!

YUSUF *(smirking)* Haha, I have a used cucumber in my room that would argue differently!

Yusuf, Paris and Ricky break into laughter. Beat.

PARIS So, do you want to take that job or not? I'll tell Dolly if you do.

RICKY Well, the money's good, but...

PARIS But what? You don't like women?

RICKY No, that's not it. *(Beat)* It just seems like a sin...

PARIS Sin? Here you are, strutting around, showing off all your assets and orifices for everyone to see... Isn't that a sin? *(looking at Yusuf)* And you, selling your body to old men. Isn't that a sin?

YUSUF *(huffily)* Excuse me, sister. Here you are, trying to be a woman when you're really a man. Isn't that a sin?

PARIS Stop this. I have to get back to Dolly. *(To Ricky)* So are you going to take the job or not?

RICKY What if it is not just a photoshoot? What if I have to have sex with an old woman. I've never had a girlfriend, never even been kissed...

Paris suddenly plops a brief kiss on Ricky's lips. Ricky looks confused.

PARIS There! At least now you can stop saying you've never been kissed! *(Beat.)*

Blackout.

INT. STARLIGHT. NIGHT

It's another night at Starlight and another round in the Miss Drag Queen competition. Again, Yusuf is dressed outlandishly and Paris looks even more feminine than before. The two are huddled together on a chaise longue engaged in small talk and sipping from cola bottles. On the coffee table before them is a drink. In the background Ricky is visible, doing a pole dance.

PARIS *(taking Yusuf's hand and putting it on his forearm)* Just feel my skin. I've been taking birth-control pills and can really tell the difference. I read on the internet that birth-control pills help to prevent hair and muscle growth.

YUSUF But if you take birth pills... *(laughing)*... you won't be able to have children!

PARIS That's alright. I don't want children. Poor things would be called names: drag baby and all... *(laughs as well)*

YUSUF Speaking of which, tonight is another round in the Miss Drag Queen contest. Why don't you join — if you're ready to compete with me, that is.

PARIS I don't want to be a drag queen. I told you, I want to be a woman, a real woman!

YUSUF Fine! Better in fact. *(laughs)* One less competitor for me.

Ricky finishes his pole dance and joins Yusuf and Paris. His body is glistening with sweat.

RICKY Whose drink is that? Can I...?

YUSUF Yours, in fact. The bartender sent it over with the message that it's from an admirer, but he didn't say which one.

Ricky takes a gulp of the drink and tries to sit down next to Paris who pushes him away.

PARIS Get away from me! You're all wet and disgusting. *(squeezing his nostrils shut)* Go to the changing room and dry yourself off.

RICKY I can't. There are people there. Front people...

PARIS Front people? The 'Morality Front'? What do they want here?

RICKY A piece of the action! I thought you knew that.

YUSUF Yeah, and I heard the boss here is a couple months behind payments to those thugs.

RICKY Those same people who raid bars and nightclubs and go on about sexy-looking celebrities are also in the business of providing protection for clubs like this one.

YUSUF For all their talk about Islam, it's just money and power they want.

PARIS God, no different from politicians!

RICKY Shit, I'm thirsty! *(He chugs the rest of the drink.)* I got to get back to work.

Ricky returns to the pole and dances more wildly and more sensually than usual.

Blackout.

INT. HOTEL ROOM. DAY

In the hotel room Ricky is sprawled on the bed, his wrists tied to the back of the bed. The room is a mess. When the telephone rings Ricky lifts his head and looks slowly around in search of the source of the sound. He yanks his arms until his bonds are released, then fumbles as he looks for his pants on the floor and his cellphone in the pocket. He punches the answer button. A voice is heard.

PARIS Hello! Where are you? We've been looking all over for you? You left last night and didn't tell us. Where did you go? *(more impatiently)* Tell me, where did you go! Say something...! Rickkkyy!

Ricky seems unable to speak. He starts to put his clothes on.

RICKY *(mumbling)* Come get me...

PARIS Where are you?

Ricky looks around at the room.

RICKY	That hotel where you brought me.
PARIS	What room?
RICKY	I don't know! Just come!

Blackout.

INT. PESANTREN. DAY

Seated on his mattress, Ricky appears to be lost in thought. Shaking his head, he then laughs and speaks to the audience.

RICKY That job offer of mine… Turns out it was just a photoshoot after all, and I got the rest of the money I needed to pay off Ustaz Asman.

Yeah, there were some nude shots, too, but Dolly promised that they were for her client's private use only. The thing that had me worried — that I would have to screw some old woman — didn't happen at all. But look at what happened: some guy, and I don't even know who, fucked me instead. Where were my special powers then?

YUSUF *(sticking his head in the door, then coming in)* Who were you talking to…? You know, Ricky, the boss at Starlight has been texting me, asking when you're coming back to work.

RICKY I've repented! I'm giving up that life.

YUSUF Repent? You didn't do anything wrong.

RICKY But maybe I did and that's why I was punished. I was raped! That must be a punishment for something!

YUSUF *(insistently)* You did nothing wrong, Ricky! And look at you like this, doing nothing but hide out in this cell. You may have paid off Ustaz Asman, but you still need money, don't you? What with Paris putting all his money aside for a sex change operation, I know he's no longer keeping you.

RICKY But maybe it's wrong, flaunting my body and all.

YUSUF Well, do you have another way of making money? *(Ricky doesn't answer.)* At the very least, you need to talk to the boss and tell him directly. *(Beat)* Plus, I want you there at the Miss

Drag Queen finals. I'm so hoping to win! I've never won anything before in my life, and if I do I want my friends to be there.

RICKY But what about you? How long do you want to do this kind of thing?

YUSUF Meaning?

RICKY How long are you going to go on dressing up like a woman and chasing after men?

YUSUF What, you think that's a sin? I don't need a lecture about sin. I've lived in this *pesantren* before I could walk. I've studied the Quran from front to back and was force-fed notions about sin long before I could lip-synch. I want to stop thinking about sin. All I want is a normal life, like other people. A home and enough means to get by. Is that a sin? *(Beat)* You're going with me, okay?!

Yanking the peci that Ricky is wearing from off Ricky's head, Yusuf throws it in his face and then turns and leaves the room.

INT. STARLIGHT. NIGHT

Ricky and Paris are at Starlight waiting for the show to begin and for Yusuf to appear. Ricky is dressed in wings and briefs. But now, around his neck, hangs an amulet.

RICKY *(to Paris)* Where's Yusuf? Huh, I mean "Yolanda"? Is he ready?

PARIS Yes, she's ready.

RICKY By the way, you look very pretty tonight.

PARIS *(blushing)* What the...? *(Beat. Looking at Ricky and stroking his wings.)* Would you look at that? The boy I once kept now has wings!

At this moment Yusuf comes out in full drag, takes his place on stage and starts to perform. All of a sudden, in the middle of his performance, the sound of "Allahu Akbar" is heard and a melee begins when members of the Moral Front stampede into the room brandishing poles, swords and knives. As they advance towards the stage Yusuf remains standing there, dumbstruck. Ricky jumps onto the stage to protect Yusuf. He pushes Yusuf to the catwalk floor and covers him with his body. A man with a machete swings the machete at Ricky but it bounces off Ricky's back and slices into Paris's chest, who is standing close by. Paris clutches his chest. In the background, Ariana Grande's "No More Tears to Cry" plays. As police sirens and whistles are heard the attacker flees. Ricky and Yusuf, still lying on the floor are unaware that Paris has been hurt. Ricky rolls off of Yusuf.

YUSUF You're not hurt?

Ricky shakes his head and tugs on his amulet. Suddenly Paris falls to the floor and begins to tremble wildly. Not knowing what to do, Ricky holds him tightly. Yusuf huddles with them too.

RICKY & YUSUF *(screaming)* Help!

Blackout.

INT. PESANTREN. DAY.

In his room Ricky is going through his things and packing a bag, but then stops what he is doing.

RICKY *(to the audience)* What was that — Paris dying — some kind of punishment from Allah? Did he deserve to die? Is what we were doing sinful or wrong?

These past months have been the happiest moments in my life — exploring the world outside of my bubble, getting to know who I really am and, finally, for the first time finding happiness with ease. Happiness was no longer a question for me. *(Beat)*

But now I have to ask, was my happiness wrong? *(shaking his head)* No... Wrong is taking away Paris from my life. Wrong is people deciding what's right or wrong for others.

It's been months since I've been to Starlight, not since that night I lost my best friend. I wonder if I'll ever find another friend like him. Maybe I will. I just don't know.

Maybe, if fate is on my side, those wings of mine that were broken that night can be repaired and can lift us up to a nest high from the ground and away from danger.

Who in the world understands?

Lights down.

The End.

Glossary

pesantren (also *pondok pesantren)* – An Islamic boarding school, but one with deep roots in Indonesia's pre-Muslim past. *Pesantren* dormitories are often very simple, almost spartan, with nothing more than a sleeping mat or mattress and a peg to hang one's clothes.

peci – An untassled fez-like hat, considered to be the national headdress for men in Indonesia; often worn by male Muslims, especially on Fridays for public prayer.

kitab kuning – (lit. yellow book), in the Islamic religious education, refers to the traditional set of the Islamic texts used by the educational curriculum of the Islamic seminary in Indonesia, especially within the madrasahs and pesantrens.

pencak silat – A kind of martial arts specific to Indonesia.

kebatinan – The practice of Javanese mysticism, including fasting and meditation, through which one is able to obtain supernatural powers.

Trisa Triandesa

Born in Bandung, 1984, from a young age he enjoyed traditional dances and traditional puppet shows (*wayang golek*). Performance arts have been an important part of his life, and that led him to learn to sing, dance, play traditional musical instruments and act while completing his studies in Psychology. After several years acting on stage and TV, he was involved in the first LGBT-themed web series in Indonesia — soon banned by the government — CONQ. He also starred in several films, including the award-winning and critically-acclaimed movie *Selamat*

Pagi, Malam (In the Absence of the Sun) by one of Indonesia's most exciting young directors, Lucky Kuswandi.

Also with an interest in writing, Trisa began by translating *Three Sisters* by Anton Chekhov into Indonesian. Later, he adapted and performed the monologue *On the Harmful Effects of Tobacco* by Anton Chekhov.

Sin is his first stage adaptation of a novel.

Other than the arts, Trisa is also involved in a lot of campaigns/social movements regarding sexual health and reproductive rights, HIV/AIDS, mental health and education issues.

Nuril Basri

Nuril Basri was born in a village in Tangerang in western Java, now in the province of Banten, in 1985. A graduate of the Islamic State University in Jakarta, Nuril has worked in a variety of positions over the years: internet café manager, secretary to a police attaché, private language tutor, mini-market cashier, and waiter on a cruise ship.

His writing spans tragicomedy and *bildungsroman* with themes around: loneliness, insecurity, friendship, dysfunctional family, LGBT, and the underdogs. His works have been translated into English and Malay. Published works include: *Halo, Aku Dalam* Novel (2009), *My Favorite Goodbye* (2015); *Sunyi* (2017); *Not a Virgin* (2017), *Love, Lies and Indomee* (Epigram, 2019), etc.

Nuril was awarded a grant by the National Book Committee of Indonesia to complete a residency in the UK in 2017. And recently received a grant from Robert Bosch Stiftung & Literarisches Colloquium Berlin 'Crossing Borders' to conduct research for his next novel in Germany. He likes funny stuff and to ride motorcycles.

John H. McGlynn

John H. McGlynn, publisher and translator of Indonesian literature, has translated several dozen publications under his own name, and through the Lontar Foundation, which he co-founded in 1987, has ushered into print close to two hundred books on Indonesian language, literature and culture. He has helped to shape the world view of Indonesian literature, almost single-handedly creating a canon of Indonesian literature in English.

www.lontar.org

BREAK IN

Agnes Christina

Characters
DAUGHTER
MOTHER
GECKO
DOOR
GIRL IN THE MIRROR
KETTLE
MAN

DAY 1, NIGHT TIME, DAUGHTER'S BEDROOM

MOTHER	Wash your feet.
DAUGHTER	Yes.
MOTHER	Don't forget to pray.
DAUGHTER	Yes.

Mother closes the door to her daughter's room. Daughter pulls up her blanket and tries to sleep. But she can't sleep. She reaches out to her telephone and calls her friend. No answer. She puts down her phone. She now stares at her ceiling; there is a gecko crawling across it.

DAUGHTER	Gecko, why are you not asleep?
GECKO	I am waiting for you to sleep.
DAUGHTER	Why do you have to wait for me?
GECKO	It is rude for me, a guest, to sleep earlier than the owner of the house.
DAUGHTER	How long have you stayed in my room?
GECKO	I came here two days ago.

DAUGHTER Why do I only see you now?

GECKO On my first day, I wandered around the floor. Second day, the wall. Today, the ceiling.

DAUGHTER I didn't even see you in the afternoon.

GECKO Well, you never watch your steps.

DAUGHTER True... are you going to stay here for long?

GECKO If I don't die quickly.

DAUGHTER Don't die quickly. I can put you in a glass jar and feed you so that you won't die.

GECKO I am used to crawling around the walls; I can't live in a glass jar. I'd die of boredom.

DAUGHTER What's your plan tomorrow?

GECKO I'm going to your mother's room.

DAUGHTER After you are done exploring her room, please come back to my room.

GECKO What for?

DAUGHTER I want to know, what does my mother do every night.

GECKO Okay! I will come back. Now can you please sleep, I want to sleep now.

DAUGHTER Okay, good night!

The daughter closes her eyes and sleeps. The gecko, now that the owner of the house is asleep, follows suit.

NIGHT 2, DAUGHTER'S ROOM

MOTHER Wash your feet.

DAUGHTER Yes

MOTHER Don't forget to pray.

DAUGHTER Yes.

Mother closes the door and switches off the light. Daughter pulls up her blanket and stares at the ceiling.

DAUGHTER Gecko?

No answer. Gecko is in Mother's room. Daughter reaches out to her telephone and calls her friend. No answer again. Daughter hugs her bolster in a foetal position facing the mirror on the wardrobe beside her bed.

DAUGHTER Gecko is in mother's room.

GIRL IN THE MIRROR He will come back when he's done making friends with Mother.

DAUGHTER How many days?

GIRL IN THE MIRROR Maybe three days... floor, walls, ceiling.

DAUGHTER But mother's room is way bigger than my room.

GIRL IN THE MIRROR Patience...

Daughter closes her eyes. She sees a black hole inside her eyelids, spinning, sucking her into the blackness.

NIGHT 3, DAUGHTER'S ROOM

MOTHER Have you washed your feet?

DAUGHTER Yes.

MOTHER Make sure you pray.

DAUGHTER Yes.

Mother leaves without closing the door. Daughter watches her mother disappear behind the walls, then she gets up, walks towards the door, closes it and sits on the floor, leaning against the door.

DAUGHTER Is Mother angry with you?

DOOR Why do you think so?

DAUGHTER She hasn't touched you tonight.

DOOR Maybe she forgets.

DAUGHTER How does it feel to be touched by her?

DOOR Warm. Your mother's fingers are always gentle and warm. Her touch is motherly.

DAUGHTER How about my fingers?

DOOR Your touch is cold. You demand warmth from me, but I can't give you any. You know very well that I am an insulator.

Daughter gets up and lays herself on the bed, but this time her back is facing the Girl in the Mirror.

GIRL IN THE MIRROR What's wrong?

DAUGHTER I am sleepy.

GIRL IN THE MIRROR Sleep, then…

Daughter closes her eyes. This time, her eyelids emit red and blue smoke. Odourless, but it makes her chest feel so tight.

NIGHT 4, DAUGHTER'S ROOM

MOTHER Wash feet.

DAUGHTER Yes.

MOTHER Pray.

DAUGHTER Yes.

Daughter turns her head towards her mother, but Mother is already gone. Daughter walks up to close the door quickly and she is about to lay on her bed, but Door starts a conversation with her.

DOOR Are you angry with me? *(Daughter turns to face the door.)* You don't wish to talk to me anymore?

DAUGHTER I never meant that…

DOOR Are you sleepy?

DAUGHTER I am never sleepy.

DOOR Then why do you sleep every night?

DAUGHTER Don't I have to?

DOOR Not really.

DAUGHTER But if I don't sleep, I won't wake up tomorrow morning.

DOOR I can stay closed when your mother comes here tomorrow.

DAUGHTER Why are you only offering your help now?

Door doesn't answer. Daughter walks closer to the door, sits on the floor and leans against the door, caressing the door softly.

DAUGHTER   How long have you stood here?
DOOR   Since this house was built.
DAUGHTER   I'm 15 years old. How old is this house?
DOOR   19 years.
DAUGHTER   We are four years apart. Mother said, four years' difference is good. Four symbolizes the legs of a table in each corner, holding up the table strongly.
DOOR   But we only started talking last night.
DAUGHTER   I'm afraid to start a conversation.
DOOR   But someone has got to start, right?
DAUGHTER   Why don't you start?
DOOR   I am shy.
DAUGHTER   Why?
DOOR   I'm scared that you are angry with me.
DAUGHTER   Why?
DOOR   I always take a peek when you change your clothes.
DAUGHTER   I don't feel spied on.
DOOR   I promise to never peek again.
DAUGHTER   Promise?
DOOR   Yes, promise.
DAUGHTER   Don't you sleep?
DOOR   I sleep in the afternoon, when you're not in this room.
DAUGHTER   Are you afraid that I will take a peek when you are asleep?
DOOR   No, I always have to guard you when you are in this room.
DAUGHTER   You are so kind.

DOOR I don't want anyone to harm you when you are asleep.

DAUGHTER Are you the boss of all the furniture in this room?

DOOR I am the king of this room. I am responsible for guarding everything inside here.

DAUGHTER Thank you.

DOOR Can I kiss your forehead?

Daughter kisses the door's cheek softly. All night, Daughter embraces the door until she falls asleep. The door stays awake, as usual, guarding everything in the room.

MORNING, DAY 5 , DAUGHTER'S ROOM

Morning comes, Mother is about to open Daughter's door, but she can't.

MOTHER Open the door!

Door doesn't want to wake his queen from her sleep. Mother tries to force open the door, but the door stays locked. Mother searches for a spare key but she can't find it.

Mother tries to call the locksmith, but the phone line was cut off.

Mother gets out of the house in panic, waiting for a truck to pass by so that she can hitch a ride.

Mother's house is on top of a hill, in the middle of a huge tea plantation. She owns no car, no motorbike, and there are no neighbours. Every Sunday, she usually hitches a ride from the truck that brings the tea leaves to the market at the foot of the hill.

Today is Monday.

After waiting for 30 minutes, she grows restless and gives up. It seems like she has to walk down the hill.

She walks down the hill to find a vehicle that can bring her to the locksmith.

And the daughter wakes up.

DAUGHTER   What time is it?

DOOR   It's ten o'clock in the morning.

DAUGHTER   What? I have to go to school.

DOOR   Today is a holiday. Don't you remember?

DAUGHTER   Oh, yes, I forgot.

DOOR   What did you dream last night?

DAUGHTER   I don't like dreams.

DOOR   Because...?

DAUGHTER   Because I never dream. I don't know what dreaming feels like. Do you dream?

DOOR   No, I don't like to daydream.

DAUGHTER   It's almost noon now. Are you sleeping already?

DOOR   I am not sleeping. I have to guard you.

DAUGHTER   I will get out from this room, then. So you don't need to worry about me.

DOOR   If you go out, I still can't sleep. Your mother is not at home. Who will guard you if not me?

DAUGHTER   Let's sleep together, then. I will accompany you sleeping.

DOOR   What will happen if I sleep and your mother opens me?

DAUGHTER   We can still chat at night.

Daughter caresses the door until both of them fall asleep. Daughter gets awoken by the noise outside. Her mother is trying to force open the door. Door wakes up, trying his best to stay locked.

DAUGHTER   Door, it's okay, just let yourself be opened.

DOOR   I have to guard you.

DAUGHTER   It must be my Mother.

DOOR   No, this is a man.

DAUGHTER   Father? But it is not time yet for him to come out of jail. He still has five more years. Door, don't let yourself be opened. I don't want to meet him now. Help me.

DOOR Yes.

DAUGHTER I will help you from here *(while pressing her weight against the door)*.

DOOR Thank you.

DAUGHTER I don't want to meet Father.

DOOR Don't be afraid.

From under the door, Gecko crawls in slowly.

GECKO Why don't you get out?

DAUGHTER I don't want to meet Father.

GECKO So that man is your father?

DAUGHTER I... I don't know... Door, is that my father?

GECKO Open the door, you'll know if it's your father or not.

DAUGHTER Door, that's my father, right?

DOOR I will do whatever you say. If you want me to stay closed, I will.

DAUGHTER So who is that man?

DOOR I don't know either.

DAUGHTER Gecko, is that my father?

GECKO I don't know. This morning your mother went out for quite a while, then comes home with this man.

DAUGHTER Is Mother crazy? How can she bring Father back here?

GECKO What's the problem?

DAUGHTER Don't pretend you don't know. You stayed for so long in Mother's room, you must know something.

GECKO Your mother didn't talk to me, so I stayed quiet.

DAUGHTER So what did you do in her room?

GECKO I crawled around and waited for her to sleep. After she goes to sleep, I sleep.

DAUGHTER What does she do every night?

GECKO Pray and sleep.

DAUGHTER That's it?
GECKO What else should she do?
DAUGHTER I don't know… phone call?
GECKO Praying is similar to having a phone call with God.
DAUGHTER No, it isn't. In a phone call, someone will answer from the other end of the line. In prayers, nobody answers you.

Door can't stand it anymore. The doorframe has already been eaten by termites. It is so fragile. As the man outside the room keeps pushing, the door falls onto Daugther and Gecko.

Daughter faints while Gecko dies flat on the floor.

The locksmith feels guilty, so he carries Daughter to his car and takes her to the hospital.

NIGHT, DAY 5, IN A HOSPITAL ROOM

MOTHER Wash your feet.
DAUGHTER Yes.

Mother wipes Daughter's feet until they are clean.

MOTHER Pray before you sleep.
DAUGHTER Yes.

Mother prays beside Daughter's bed. Daughter observes her mother praying; her mouth keeps moving, making inaudible sounds. Mother opens her eyes, her eyes meet her Daughter's eyes.

MOTHER You didn't pray? *(Daughter stays quiet.)* That's why the door fell on to you. You never pray! God is angry with you because you never call Him.
DAUGHTER My call is never answered.
MOTHER How do you know that God never answers your call?
DAUGHTER I don't get any reply. I'd rather talk to Gecko, to the door, to the mirror. They do answer me.

Mother lays down on the sofa beside Daughter's bed, closing her eyes.

DAUGHTER   What did you talk about with Gecko last night?
MOTHER   Which gecko?
DAUGHTER   The one who has been in your room for two days.
MOTHER   There are so many geckos in our house.
DAUGHTER   Are you really angry with Door?
MOTHER   How do I get angry with Door?
DAUGHTER   Why did you force open the door?
MOTHER   I forced it open because it couldn't be opened. And why did you have to stand behind the door? You knew very well that someone outside was trying to open it.
DAUGHTER   I don't want to meet Father.
MOTHER   Me neither.
DAUGHTER   Door said he wants to protect me from Father.
MOTHER   Just lock the door. Father can't get in if it is locked.
DAUGHTER   Father won't be staying with us anymore, right?
MOTHER   I have changed the lock to our house. He won't be able to get in. He doesn't have the key.
DAUGHTER   What if somebody inside brings him in?
MOTHER   In our house, there is only me and you. If you think that geckos, doors and mirrors are "somebody inside", by all means, be suspicious towards them.
DAUGHTER   Door said Father was trying to force him open.
MOTHER   What?
DAUGHTER   That's why he refused to be opened.
MOTHER   Why did you never tell me?
DAUGHTER   Seems that somebody from inside brought Father in.
MOTHER   Who is somebody inside? There is no one else in our house except me and you!

DAUGHTER	Now that Gecko is dead, I have no one to trust anymore.
MOTHER	Stop it! I am tired talking to you. I sent you to school so that you could have friends, but you prefer to have geckos, door and mirrors as friends. You are 15 years old. It is not the age to have imaginary friends anymore.
DAUGHTER	I'm able to talk with them. They can be trusted more than you.
MOTHER	Fine! You don't need to talk to me anymore if you don't trust me.
DAUGHTER	I never talk to you, do I? You only talk to me when you ask me to wash my feet and to pray. Your definition of talking is strange!
MOTHER	Go to sleep. I am tired.

Daughter stares at the ceiling looking for Gecko, but it is not there. The hospital is too clean. She closes her eyes.

DAUGHTER   God, I give you one chance. If you don't answer me, I will never talk to You ever again. I want to see Gecko.

No response. Daughter sleeps with a grudge.

MORNING. DAY 6, AT THE LAKESIDE

In the morning when Daughter wakes up, she is beside a lake with blue water. It is a misty but dry area. There is an old hut nearby. She walks up to the hut and opens its door without knocking. The hut is empty. There is only a table, a chair and a kettle on the table.

KETTLE	Don't you have any manners?
DAUGHTER	I thought this hut was empty.
KETTLE	So what are we? Dead objects? *(Daughter keeps quiet.)* I am the master of the hut. You have to greet me before you enter. At least, you could knock on the door.
DAUGHTER	Okay. Excuse me, I would like to sit here for a while.

KETTLE Yes, have a seat. Do you want to drink?

DAUGHTER Thank you. I am thirsty.

KETTLE What brings you here?

DAUGHTER I was asleep, and when I opened my eyes, I was at the lakeside, then I saw this hut.

KETTLE Oh, usual story.

DAUGHTER Am I dreaming?

KETTLE You think?

DAUGHTER Yes, I think I am dreaming. I was sleeping in the hospital.

KETTLE How can you say that the hospital is the reality and this hut is a dream? It could be the other way round.

DAUGHTER But I have lived in that world with a hospital in it for 15 years.

KETTLE Maybe you have been asleep at the lakeside for 15 years.

DAUGHTER Impossible for me to sleep that long. I am never sleepy.

KETTLE Of course you are never sleepy. You've been sleeping here for fifteen years.

DAUGHTER Hmm...

KETTLE Don't worry, you can take a walk outside. The scenery is beautiful.

DAUGHTER What is the name of this place?

KETTLE Lakeside.

DAUGHTER How far is my house from here?

KETTLE I don't know. I can't walk. Everyday I just sit on this table.

DAUGHTER Is there anyone else staying in this hut?

KETTLE There is.

DAUGHTER Why is he not here?

KETTLE He is outside, looking for his daughter and wife. It's been five days since he went out. He should be back here today.

DAUGHTER How do you know that he'll be back today? Did you make a phone call?

KETTLE Communication doesn't always have to be a phone call.

DAUGHTER Telepathy?

KETTLE Similar, but different.

DAUGHTER How does it work?

KETTLE You trust him, he trusts you. You know each other well for years. Before you know it, you'll notice what is happening in his life, and he knows what's on your mind.

DAUGHTER So... you have a hunch that he'll come back today?

KETTLE Yes, I know he got into an accident yesterday, so he should be back here today.

DAUGHTER So this is the afterlife?

KETTLE This is the lakeside!

DAUGHTER But if dead people come here, then this is the afterlife.

KETTLE Did I say that he died? I only said he got into an accident.

DAUGHTER So this is a hospital?

KETTLE You surely lack imagination, don't you?

DAUGHTER My mother said, I am at the age where I have to stop imagining things.

KETTLE Your mother sounds boring.

DAUGHTER Very.

KETTLE No wonder her husband left her...

DAUGHTER How do you know about that?

KETTLE You are annoying as well. You deserve to be left alone.

DAUGHTER But the door cares about me a lot. So does Gecko and the Girl in the Mirror...

KETTLE He-he-he.

Daughter realizes that the only real communication in her life is with non-humans.

DAUGHTER   I'm going...
KETTLE   Where to?
DAUGHTER   To find human beings. Mother was right. I am too old to have imaginary friends.
KETTLE   Wait a little longer... the other master of the hut is almost here...
DAUGHTER   What master? For this silly old hut, the most you can get for a master is a gecko!
KETTLE   There, you've said it! Sit down. Wait till he comes. You have to thank him – you have drunk his water.
DAUGHTER   Okay, I will wait for a while. After I say thank you, I will leave.
KETTLE   As you wish...

They wait for the gecko's arrival. The door opens by itself. Daughter is surprised and looks at the door. There is nobody. She slowly walks to the door....

DAUGHTER   There is no one here...
KETTLE   You never watch your step. How can you see?

Daughter looks down, Gecko is there.

DAUGHTER   Gecko!! I thought you were dead!
GECKO   He-he-he.
DAUGHTER   So this is your house? I drank your water!
GECKO   I know, kettle told me.
DAUGHTER   Let's go back home. Kettle can come along with us.
GECKO   No no no, I don't want to be flattened out again.
DAUGHTER   Oh well...
GECKO   Hmm... anyway, I don't know the way back to your house.
DAUGHTER   So how do I get back home?
GECKO   I think... you don't need to go home.

DAUGHTER But Mother will look for me...
GECKO Are you sure?
DAUGHTER Of course! Who else will accompany her home?
GECKO Your father?

Daughter falls silent. She remembers the moment when Door was forced open. There was a man behind it.

DAUGHTER So Mother doesn't want me anymore?

Daughter runs to the lake and lays down on the same spot that she woke up earlier. Gecko climbs on the tree above where the daughter lays down.

DAUGHTER I know you are not a gecko.
GECKO What is the meaning of a shape?
DAUGHTER And I am not human.
GECKO How about your mother?
DAUGHTER I really don't know.
GECKO If you can shapeshift, what do you want to become?
DAUGHTER I want to disappear without trace.
GECKO Even if you die, your soul stays in the lives of people that you have touched.
DAUGHTER I know. That's why I always try to minimize contact with other people.
GECKO Your soul stays in your mother's...
DAUGHTER I came out from her womb, so technically all of me is hers. Let her take back whatever is left of me.
GECKO But you said your mother doesn't want you anymore...
DAUGHTER I don't know. I really don't know her...
GECKO Talk to her. Make a phone call.
DAUGHTER I don't know what to talk about with her.

GECKO You are funny. You've lived with your mother for fifteen years and yet you don't know what to talk about...? What will the neighbours say?

DAUGHTER I don't have any neighbours.

GECKO Ah yes, I forgot about that...

DAUGHTER Kettle told me that you were looking for your wife and daughter. Did you manage to find them?

GECKO Oh what a telltale kettle.... Yes, I have found them, but my business is not done yet.

DAUGHTER So you will visit them again? Can I come along?

GECKO Of course! They've been living in your house all this while.

DAUGHTER In my room? Or in Mother's room?

GECKO Mother's room.

DAUGHTER No wonder Mother was saying there are lots of geckos in our house.

GECKO Your mother is so observant. We can't hide from her.

DAUGHTER Mother has a hundred eyes, I think. Nothing escapes her observation other than me. She doesn't notice me, she doesn't know me at all.

GECKO Of course she doesn't know you; you never even talk to her!

DAUGHTER What does she pray about every night?

GECKO Prayers are your secret with God; it's a private matter.

DAUGHTER I am just confused. How can she never run out of topics to talk about with God? Does she repeat the same prayer every night?

GECKO When was your last time praying?

DAUGHTER Before I went to sleep last night. Actually, it was my first time.

GECKO Wow! I am amazed! Fifteen years and only one prayer.

DAUGHTER I just feel that it's not important. I don't even know what God looks like or where God is. How can God reply to my call? I don't know God's phone number.

GECKO What is the meaning of a shape? *(Daughter keeps quiet again.)* So, you think this lake is reality or a dream? Or the afterlife? Or...?

DAUGHTER Gecko, how did you get into my house? You said you don't know the way there.

GECKO What is the meaning of a place? What's important is that we can communicate, right?

Daughter thinks hard.

DAUGHTER If place is not important, that means... I'm confused! I want to see my mother! I don't want her to be angry with me!

GECKO Trust me. What is the meaning of a place? What's important is communication. That's why Kettle can communicate with me even though we are in different places.

DAUGHTER I think I'm still in the hospital now. Is this a hallucination?

GECKO Ahh... don't make assumptions...

DAUGHTER Wait a minute... if a place is not important and the most important thing is communication... I think you are the key, Gecko!

GECKO I can't shapeshift into a key...

DAUGHTER At home and in this lakeside, we can talk. What's the meaning of a place! What's the meaning of a shape!

GECKO I think you've got it.

DAUGHTER We can talk in the hospital as well...

GECKO I think we are in the hospital...

MORNING. DAY 6, IN THE HOSPITAL

Daughter turns her head to her right side. Her mother is still asleep on the sofa. She looks up at the ceiling. Gecko is not there.

DAUGHTER   Mother, when can I go home?

Mother slowly opens her eyes.

MOTHER   Doctor said there is no serious injury, only bruises. This afternoon we can go home.

DAUGHTER   Has the door in my room been repaired?

MOTHER   Oh, how could I forget... I should have asked the locksmith to repair it. After all, he was the one who forced it open. I'll call him when we get home.

DAUGHTER   Huh? So it was the locksmith who pushed open the door? Not Father?

MOTHER   Why should Father push open your door? Your father is a prisoner, not a locksmith. He can't help me open your door.

DAUGHTER   I thought it was Father. That's why I kept the door closed.

MOTHER   Why did you think that it was your father?

DAUGHTER   Door said there was a man outside my room. And Gecko said you left the house for quite a while and came back with that man. I thought you fetched Father from the prison.

MOTHER   That's why you'd better talk to your mother, not to the door or to the gecko.

DAUGHTER   Ahh... what is the meaning of a shape? What's important is communication.

NIGHT 6, AT HOME.

Daughter's room is still a mess. The door is still on the floor. Daughter walks around the door and picks up her blanket.

GIRL IN THE MIRROR You have bruises all over your body.

DAUGHTER Maybe this is God's punishment because I never pray to Him.

GIRL IN THE MIRROR Are you going to pray tonight?

DAUGHTER I started praying last night.

GIRL IN THE MIRROR So you have made friends with God?

DAUGHTER You could say so…

GIRL IN THE MIRROR What do you pray for?

DAUGHTER Prayer is a private matter…

Daughter walks out of her room. The Girl in the Mirror follows her out of her room.

Daughter stops by the door and caresses it.

DAUGHTER Door, today I will be sleeping in Mother's room.

DOOR I can't protect you anymore. I am down.

DAUGHTER Don't be sad, Door. You are meant to be opened and closed. Yesterday morning we were wrong. It was as if we rejected our fate and closed ourselves from what we are supposed to do. You are supposed to be opened and closed. If we want to stay closed, we can be walls.

DOOR Have a good night.

DAUGHTER Door, I'd like to know. Why didn't you say that it wasn't my father?

DOOR I was only following your heart.

DAUGHTER What do you mean?

DOOR Your heart asked me to stay closed. So I didn't let myself be opened.

DAUGHTER How can you know what my heart wants?

DOOR I can read it from the beat of your heart. I know you.

DAUGHTER Thank you, Door. You are a truly great king that understands everything in this room. Have a good rest… Tonight, Mother will take care of me.

DOOR I will rest well…

DAUGHTER   Good night, Door.

Daughter kisses the door and walks to her mother's room. Door slowly closes his eyes and smiles. Before entering her mother's room, Daughter washes her feet.

MOTHER   Have you washed your feet?
DAUGHTER   I have.
MOTHER   Now let's pray before we sleep.
DAUGHTER   Yes.

Mother and Daughter pray and sleep till the sun rises.

The End.

Agnes Christina

Agnes is a multidisciplinary artist who is interested in the struggle that people face in life, and most importantly how they deal with the struggle. Focusing on the rhythm that is created by humans in everyday life, Agnes presents her findings mostly through performances that collaborate with other media such as film and painting.

In 2013, Agnes received an eighteen month research and creation residency, the Substation Directors' Lab Programme from the National Arts Council Singapore, where she conducted research on Serat Centhini, the most magnificent Javanese traditional literature, which is the Javanese encyclopedia of life, and she presented it in a series of performances.

In 2012, she received a Hotwave residency from Cemeti Art House, which was supported by the Netherlands Embassy and Heden, in which she presented an interactive multimedia performance titled *Tukang Gosip* as her response to the social life in Yogyakarta.

Translator's note:

For audiences who may not be aware of ongoing ethnic conflicts in Indonesia, I have chosen to insert specificity not present in the original Indonesian version of the play, such as adding a cast list, including the ethnicity of the characters, indicating a location in the setting, linking the significance of sunset to evening Muslim prayers, etc.

It is important to note that the playwright had intentionally left out the specificity that I added; local Indonesian audiences would understand the ethnic and religious cues through casting, regional accents and familiarity with actual historical events and ongoing conflicts similar to those represented in the play.

While the play tackles universal themes of forbidden love, religious profiteering, misogyny, corruption and more, I believe that having an understanding of the context in which the source operates helps to enrich the experience of it in translation.

BEDFELLOWS

Hanna Fransisca

Translated by Cobina Gillitt

Characters

All characters are ethnically Chinese-Indonesian unless mentioned otherwise.

SELMA owner of the coffee shop, married to Tom, 30 years old
MR. GOEN pimp running a child trafficking outfit that arranges marriages of local ethnic Chinese girls to Taiwanese men
SIMPO Mr. Goen's associate, in his late 40s
LINGLING new recruit engaged to a Taiwanese man, 14 years old
RIKA waitress, 13 years old
NANI waitress, young teenager
MARWAN Muslim activist, ethnically Malay
SUDIN Muslim activist, ethnically Malay
TOM Selma's husband, owner of an inn

Setting

A town with a large Chinese-Indonesian community, located in the province of West Kalimantan, Indonesia, a majority Muslim country. The front room of a coffee shop located on the corner of a main intersection.

Time

Early 21st century

Late afternoon just before the call to Maghreb (sunset) Muslim prayers. The shop is mostly deserted. Simpo and Mr. Goen sit at a table with Lingling. The men are engaged in serious discussion.

Selma sits at the cash register, reading. From time to time, she casually looks over towards the customers and eavesdrops without really paying attention.

A written announcement hangs on the shop door. It reads: "With apologies to our customers, the coffee shop will close at 7:00 pm during the World Cup."

SIMPO *(pointing towards the intersection)* Take a good look at the Naga Statue standing proudly in the centre of the intersection. Ooh, here, look from here. Come on, look carefully. What's wrong with that statue? Think about it. It's truly outrageous! Truly out of bounds...

MR. GOEN Out of bounds. Out of bounds. Out of what bounds? *(laughs)* Just let them talk. Mr. Tom can always rebuild the statue after it's destroyed. Not there, obviously, but on the temple grounds. Not in the middle of an intersection like that. Now, who would dare demolish a statue in the temple courtyard? *(holds his head and laughs. Speaks loudly towards Selma, trying to get her attention.)* Isn't that right?

Selma remains indifferent and continues reading. Mr. Goen continues in a whisper.

MR. GOEN Ah, it appears the proprietress is pretending not to listen.

Lingling has been fussing with a small mirror, applying lipstick, alternating between puckering her lips and smiling.

LINGLING Where's the Taiwanese guy who's gonna be my husband? Hasn't he arrived yet?

MR. GOEN Soon. Don't speak so loudly.

SELMA *(momentarily lowers her book)* Got some new recruits, do you Mr. Goen? Don't forget the commission. If none, I could go make a report, you know...

MR. GOEN Don't be like that. *(laughs)* Nothing that could be called a recruit. I'm only involved in legal dealings. Everything I do is solely for the benefit of our town. Nothing that could be termed a recruit. Not at all. *(laughs)*

SELMA But the news is non-stop, Mr. Goen. Nowadays, everyone can talk openly about what's going on, you know what I mean? Just be careful, okay.

MR. GOEN Oh, don't trust the news. That kind of news has always been floating around. You know news hasn't been trustworthy for ages. It's true what I'm saying, right? I'm always right.

SELMA They say the deliberations have led to a decision. Taiwanese men can no longer waltz into town and leave with some random wife. Not to mention unripe ones. How old is she, Mr. Goen?

LINGLING *(puts down her mirror)* Hey, don't be dissing me. Easy for you to say, unripe. Look, take a look. *(caresses her breasts and spins around)* Ask Mr. Goen, was I unripe last night?

MR. GOEN Hush. You be quiet. Don't talk so much. *(turns towards Selma)* Don't believe her antics! *(laughs)* She's already 18. Completely legal. Her parents don't claim her as a dependent. She already has her own ID card. And her own welfare card. I always do what's best for this town. So what was the deliberative consensus? As I just explained, it's all fake news. Exaggerated. The truth is that this town is prospering, isn't that right? *(tries to change the subject)* And the statue, what about the Naga State built and paid for by your husband, Mr. Tom. What does the news say? What's the consensus on that?

LINGLING Last night Mr. Goen said I was ripe. Seasoned, even. I am ready to perform my duties, if that Taiwanese guy ever shows up...

MR. GOEN *(whispers threateningly)* Can you not be quiet? I'll cancel your marriage to the Taiwanese gentleman if you don't shut up, understand? *(glances over towards Selma)* So what's the latest news about the Naga Statue? You must have gotten some leaked secrets from Mr. Tom. Am I right?

SIMPO The deliberative consensus is that the Naga Statue must be demolished. *(takes a deep breath, appears concerned)* Deliberative consensus, deliberative consensus, deliberative consensus. A flimsy deliberative consensus. Consensus based on what? If they only listen to the protests brought by one group of people while the others are too afraid to come forward and remain silent, how can that be considered any kind of consensus reached by deliberation?

MR. GOEN *(looks around)* Be careful what you say Simpo! Anything can happen in this kind of situation.

SIMPO *(turns towards Selma, loudly)* What's your opinion? Do you understand the meaning of the decision? This flimsy deliberative consensus?

LINGLING Why isn't he here yet? Even if I get married to the Taiwanese guy, I'm still gonna come by here from time to time. I promised to keep servicing Mr. Goen and Mr. Simpo in secret. There's no way I'll forget my promise. Mr. Goen, what does the Taiwanese guy look like? Definitely handsome, and clearly super rich. Mr. Goen, do you think the Taiwanese guy will be able to tell I'm not a virgin? 'Cause I already lost my virginity to you, Mr. Goen. What happens if my future husband finds out?

SIMPO *(to Mr. Goen)* So what? Are you scared Mr. Goen? *(louder)* Go ahead, ask her whether Tom, her husband, was ever consulted? Isn't he the one who financed the construction of the Naga Statue, the statue that at first caused such an uproar but that has now become the pride of our town?

Mr. Goen runs fearfully to the shop entrance, looks up and down the street. He then returns with a look of relief on his face.

MR. GOEN No need to talk so loudly. If there's just one, keep in mind, just one of that lot hears you talking like that, the whole mob will show up. They'll march, dispatch a motorcycle convoy around town *(stands and mimes revving up a motorcycle)*, and end up here, at this shop. At Selma's shop. And this place will be utterly destroyed, demolished. Finished.

LINGLING But Mr. Goen, you didn't lie, right? Isn't that right Mr. Goen? I've added it up, I serviced you thirty-two times. Don't forget. And that doesn't even include Mr. Simpo. I'll tell Nyonya Selma if this Taiwanese guy doesn't show up. So that she can report it.

SIMPO Ah, give it a rest. I'm done with the aggravation. Let the police actually do their work for once. This town has been peaceful for too long. I'm sick and tired of pointing out the recklessness. "O people of the city, our ancestors built everything equitably. They built temples, built churches, built mosques." In my almost fifty years of life, I had never witnessed young people get so riled up over an issue that they ended up marching on the main roads and burning down stores. Never! Even when ethnic riots erupted in all those other cities. But it had never happened here, and all the Chinese, indigenous Dayak and Malays know it. Looks like now, in my few remaining years, I'm going to witness this town abandoned by the blessings of our ancestors. Take a look *(points towards the other side of the intersection):* the Earth Deity Temple, where we all pray, won't be able to prevent the mob from tearing down the Naga Statue standing ten metres in front of it. Any respect is gone. So even if, yes, even if yes, the Naga Statue is demolished and then rebuilt on the temple grounds...Will the town gods and ancestral spirits intervene? Even I believe they haven't been present here for a long time.

LINGLING The first time at Mr. Goen's house, he said, "Don't worry Lingling, Taiwanese men are stupid, they can't tell the difference between girls who are virgins and who aren't... they're all like that. They need training to be smart."

MR. GOEN *(snarls softly in a half-whisper)* Damn it! Can't you shut your mouth? The Taiwanese gentleman will be arriving soon. *(To Selma)* Have you been listening to what Simpo's been saying?

SELMA I've only heard what Lingling has been saying.

LINGLING There you go, even she knows that Mr. Goen and Mr. Simpo have been with me thirty-two times? Yesterday, Mr. Goen told me to never tell Nyonya Selma, but if, for example, she overhears something herself, it's not my fault, right?

MR. GOEN Waitress! Bring some cake. *(glares at Lingling)* You'd better watch it if you speak again. *(laughs at Simpo)* It's not as bad as all that, Simpo! Hey, you know why the Earth Deity Temple can't stop the mob from knocking down the Naga Statue? *(glances at Selma and speaks softly)* It's because the head of the Naga Statue faces left, towards Mr. Tom's inn. Yo, you brave enough to ask Madam Selma about that? Huh? It should – Look, I'm being serious here, Simpo, I've never been more serious than this: it should... the Naga Statue should face the temple. But why is it that the head of the Naga Statue faces towards Mr. Tom's inn? Yo, you brave enough to ask? Go, ask.

Simpo frowns. Rika, who recently began waitressing at the shop, approaches the table carrying a plate of cakes.

MR. GOEN Hey, what's your name, pretty girl? Wow, wow, wow, I just noticed. When did you start working here? Hey, here, come here. *(He pulls Rika's arm, forcing her into the corner.)* So now you work here. Wow, wow, you're quite beautiful for a Chinese girl. What village are you from? Huh, quite a stroke of luck. So, what's your name? Listen up, *(whispers)* two men from Taiwan are about to arrive any moment now. You want to live the good life, right? Ho-ho-ho-ho-ho. There's no way you want to just waitress here, ho-ho-ho-ho. Surely you want to go to Taiwan like so many of your friends have already and return home a rich woman. Right? Of course you do. All the Chinese girls in town want to. Well, here's your opportunity. Op.por.tun.ity. You can become a Taiwanese wife without having to apprentice like that one *(points at Lingling)*. Listen up, ho-ho-ho-ho-ho, not every Chinese girl gets a free chance like this, ho-ho-ho-ho. You want to, right? If you are interested, you'd have to stay at my place, but only for one week. By next week, you'll be able to marry a man like one who'll be arriving here any moment. So, what's your name?

RIKA *(confused, glances fearfully at Selma)* But, I only just turned 13.

MR. GOEN Ah, the age thing isn't a problem. *(points at Lingling)* You see that girl I brought? She just turned 14!

Mr. Goen and Rika continue whispering inaudibly. Meanwhile, Simpo gets up and crosses over to Selma who stops reading.

SIMPO   Honestly, my thoughts are getting all mixed up. Please answer me this, why does the head of the Naga Statue face towards Mr. Tom's inn? Truthfully, until yesterday, I had never given it a second thought. But now my mind is suddenly laser-focused on it. This is the issue. Shouldn't the head of the Naga Statue face in the direction of the Earth Deity Temple? My apologies in advance, but the reasons behind this crucial mystery might agitate me. Is the purpose to create, sorry, fengshui? If that's its purpose, then I decidedly disapprove. Please tell me if I'm on the right track.

SELMA   That's none of my business.

SIMPO   There's no way Mr. Tom built it that way without a specific purpose. Don't forget, Mr. Tom is your husband. Surely Mr. Tom chats with you. You must also have a stake in this. What would be the point of becoming Mr. Tom's wife if you didn't have some sort of arrangement? What do you know?

SELMA   I have never been involved in any of my husband's business affairs. Understand?

SIMPO   But shouldn't...

SELMA   I do whatever I want. Everyone knows that. I own this shop, legitimately, in the clear, without anyone's intervention. And this is my life. Understand?

Simpo looks at Lingling. Shakes his head.

SIMPO *(calls out for a waitress)* Make one strong, dark coffee. No sugar. Remember, no sugar!

Mr. Goen and Rika continue to whisper inaudibly in the corner. Selma looks annoyed, puts down her book, and raps on the table with her fist. The Maghreb (sunset) Muslim call to prayer is heard softly in the distance. The music on television grows louder.

Selma barks at the waitress Nani, who sits behind the storefront.

SELMA   Turn off the TV!

Two youthful ethnic Malay Muslim men, Marwan and Sudin, arrive through the shop entrance. They both laugh loudly and then sit in chairs not too far from Simpo and Lingling's table.

Nani crosses over to Marwan and Sudin to take their order.

Mr. Goen stops his quiet conversation with Rika and hurries back to his chair. He nervously checks his watch again and again.

Nani delivers two coffees to Marwan and Sudin.

SELMA   Esteemed gentlemen. Please keep in mind the announcement hanging on the entrance door. This shop will be closing at 7:00 pm during the World Cup. That means you gentlemen have one hour left. Thus, I once again remind you of the notification. Thank you.

MARWAN *(laughs)* This Selma is really wack! I mean, we've just arrived. Oh, oh, I get it, she's such a fanatic soccer fan, she shuts down her shop. *(To Selma)* Why don't we just watch it all together? Portugal is playing North Korea tonight, a guaranteed full house. Everyone will drink and eat a lot, and you'll be lucky twice over: you can watch and make money at the same time. Whaddya think? Good suggestion, right? Who are you rooting for? Portugal or North Korea?

SELMA   I'm not rooting for either, and I don't care for soccer. That's why I'm closing the shop.

LINGLING *(to Mr. Goen)* You said 5:00 pm. And what's up with that waitress? Are you thinking of using that ugly thing instead of me? Take a good look, what is there more beautiful than me? I could cry Mr. Goen. Remember, I've already trained with you thirty-two times. Thirty. Two. Times. And that doesn't include Mr. Simpo. If I'm pushed too far, I'll report it to Nyonya Selma. I saw how scared you were earlier about her finding out.

SIMPO *(to Lingling)* Hey, you're a real blabbermouth. Shut your trap! *(looks over at the newly arrived Muslim men and then speaks softly to Mr. Goen)* It's conclusive, Mr. Tom wanted to profit from the direction of the Naga Statue head. He wanted to redirect the fengshui from the Earth Deity Temple. Imagine, the entire flow of good fortune emanating from the radiating powers of the Earth Deity Temple, captured through the tail of the Naga Statue and then directed entirely towards his inn! Imagine, the whole town's nourishing winds sourced from the Earth Deity

Temple! Obviously this is cheating! Why then have we been so proud of this Naga Statue and considered it a symbol of our town? Oh, damn it, we're doomed. Clear and convincing evidence. We've been misguided while paying homage to our ancestors. Damn it, damn it.

MR. GOEN *(surprised)* Hey, what are you talking about, Simpo? So, she said that?

SIMPO Correct. She said that to me.

SELMA Simpo is the one who said it. It wasn't me. And I don't care what he says. Let me remind you once again. When it comes to business, my husband and I are each in charge of our own affairs, without any interference. So you guys can say whatever you want, I don't care.

MARWAN *(to Selma)* Why has the TV been turned off? Don't worry or be afraid. I guarantee nothing will happen.

SELMA It's not about being afraid, Marwan. This shop already had set rules long before the riots led to shops being burned down. The television has always been turned off whenever there's the call to prayer. Haven't you guys been regulars here for years? Why is it when there's some touchy incident, all of a sudden, ordinary issues are linked to it as if they were unusual. You guys are truly weird.

MARWAN *(laughs)* Yeah, yup. Lately our town has definitely been getting weirder. *(He stands up and crosses over towards the cash register. To Selma)* Have you heard that tomorrow morning, at the height of the Cheng Beng ritual, a group is planning a motorcycle convoy on all the main roads in town as a show of strength? I'm worried their final stop will be in front of the temple with their sights set on tearing down the Naga Statue. Have you heard anything about this?

SIMPO *(whispers)* See, it's true what I said, right? The statue's destruction has been confirmed. I can now come to a definitive conclusion taking into account Mr. Tom's fraudulent plan behind the fengshui direction of the Naga's head.

Lights fade to black. Spot up on a corner focusing on Marwan and Selma, who appears calm.

MARWAN   I'm just worried Selma. Stay calm. It's a hunch, not a sure thing.

SELMA *(haltingly)* Hmm, so tomorrow morning there will be a motorcycle gang forming a convoy passing my shop, and your hunch tells you that, before arriving at the Naga Statue, they'll stop here? Is that correct, Marwan?

MARWAN   Just a hunch Selma, nothing for sure. Yeah, the situation is getting more complicated. Aha! Today you're wearing a purple shirt, isn't that the shirt... yeah, yeah, is there something worrying you, Selma? Recently I've heard...

SELMA   Tom and I are just fine.

MARWAN   Yeah, okay, fine.

Marwan and Selma fall silent.

MARWAN *(begins crooning softly)*

At a turn in the road, deep rooted trees.

Sunlight falls on the rocks.

My China Girl, dressed in purple

Sees light on the other side of skepticism.

SELMA *(closes eyes, nervously)* Can you stop with your delirious ravings Marwan? You've always assumed I'm stuck standing in the corner of my own house, just standing and looking at an expansive room that doesn't belong to me. Isn't that what you're thinking right now? Ahem. There's nothing wrong, Marwan. At least not until today. *(Selma stands and paces back and forth.)* Every decision concerning my life was initiated entirely by me. So don't ever say that I hate it. Everyone has the opportunity to make choices, and isn't there...

MARWAN   ...isn't there fate, palm lines on every hand, reincarnation into another life after death, karma, and what else Selma? Ha, this is what I keep coming back to: will there be a possibility in our next life? Oh, oh, it appears there's something else I forgot. Hold on, let me take a look. *(He moves in closer.)* Aha, a new wrinkle has appeared under your eye, Selma. I've noticed it for the past month. Yeah, yeah, who would have thought that turn in the road towards an alternate path was no more than a delusion.

SELMA *(laughs)* At least there were some moments of happiness. Those weren't delusions. Not everyone experiences moments of perfect happiness, because they usually only remember the feelings of defeat and suffering that come at the end. So most people feel lost, like failures, and that afterwards there's nothing meaningful left. Is that what you are alleging, that it was a mistake? *(Beat)* What did you say? For the past month?

MARWAN Yeah, I've noticed it for about a month.

SELMA And you know that I'm just fine, right?

MARWAN That's the reason why I asked.

SELMA Believe it. I'm fine. Every morning I open the shop without fail and always close on time. If you watched me when I open the shop, you'd know how happy it makes me to see the sunlight come streaming in, caressing the windows, warming the tables. Life goes on, Marwan. *(Beat)* How's your wife?

MARWAN Hamidah. Yeah, yeah, not all men are as lucky as I am. When I get up in the middle of the night for some reason or other, all I want is to get back to see Hamidah's face. Can you imagine Selma, after years seeing that face every day. There's always something thrilling seeing how a woman sleeps, and that delicate, sublimely beautiful woman is my wife. Like a picture composed of heavenly flowers. I feel the flow of happiness in Hamidah's breath. Then I look at her bosom, a bosom I have, of course, memorized every curve and guarded secret, but sometimes I panic and gently wake her. What do we really know about what goes on between two humans who have seen each other naked in the middle of the night? Every now and then, they are bound to question, secretly in their heads, of course: who are you really, oh freak, who for some reason or another, sleeps by my side every night? These thoughts always make me laugh, and I'm sure they would make Hamidah laugh too. *(Beat)* Anyway, if you're asking how Hamidah is, the answer is she's obviously just fine.

SELMA Tom and I often go out in the middle of the night just to sit in the park where we first met. He really is a strange man.

He constantly seeks reassurance by asking the same question: Do you love me Selma? Of course I answer that I love him. *(laughs)* Foolishness that's easy to forgive. I like the way Tommy creates a cheerful mood for our evening outings. And you can guess where it leads to from there, right? We make love until the morning, like wild horses. Often, I have to say, "Enough Tommy, enough, I have to open the shop. It's already morning!" *(laughs)* Truly, there aren't that many men as stupid as Tommy who do the same thing year after year. But his kind of stupidity, as you know Marwan, is just foolishness that's easily forgiven. There was one time when he didn't want to stop, so I asked, "Is today the day you eat lizards, Tommy?" He didn't answer, but of course he didn't need to, you know Marwan, I had so much fun asking it.

MARWAN *(doubling up with laughter)* You didn't meet up with Tommy in the park. Especially in the flower garden. Most likely those nights you brought Tommy to his father's table, where Tom whined, pleading with his father to buy off your family. *(laughs)*

SELMA *(laughing)* Are you having me on, Marwan?

MARWAN *(croons)*

> Two trees grow off the beaten path,
> Different seeds, different colours.
> When both begin to flower,
> The sun falls on the rocks.

SELMA

> The sun falls on the rocks,
> The same glow, caressing the same leaf,
> The same sun, two logs off the beaten path,
> Under the sky, loving embrace.

MARWAN *(laughs)* Turns out you still remember, Selma.

SELMA Of course I remember Marwan. Keep in mind what I said, not everyone has experienced moments of perfect happiness.

MARWAN Yeah, yeah, and it's a happiness for which we should be grateful in order to forget an ending that is unforgettable.

Is that the direction you're heading? I already know this Selma, you've gone over it many times.

Lights slowly rise onstage. All characters are visible. Sudin, who has been sitting at the table with his coffee, stands up and walks over to Marwan and Selma, who are both laughing.

Sudin pulls on Marwan's arm, leading him towards the shop exit.

SUDIN What did you leak to her?

MARWAN I don't understand what you mean by "leak." What's the deal?

SUDIN Are you nuts? I saw you whispering. Didn't we pledge not to divulge any information about this really important action?

MARWAN Hey, hold on 'Din, what do you mean by "we"? And "really important action," really important action, important for whom? For you? For who else?

SUDIN We agreed, Marwan!

MARWAN Hey, hey, heed my words. Don't ever include "me" when saying the word "we," okay? I've said this many times already, I have nothing to do with any of these plans. It's stupid, Sudin, stupid.

SUDIN Damn it Marwan. What do you mean? Are you saying that we're stupid?

MARWAN Hey, look, look at her *(nods head towards Selma)* look at her face carefully. What's wrong with her? Consider this whole town, from the time we were kids, from all our friends, from all our neighbours, school teachers, people we know, and then the entire area. What's wrong with any of it? It all points to one thing: that this town has never experienced any kind of riot or protest. That is, until the idea of forming a motorcycle convoy is proposed and the leader makes a fiery pronouncement that the convey idea is important in order to demonstrate the power of religion. Whose religion? And then you, your ranting self, leading a noisy mob to disrupt the main roads, with the feeble roar of revving motorcycles that's basically useless. And that's what you boldly call "an important action"? It's doomed. Truly dreadful Sudin! Who then, is responsible when someone yells out "Burn Shop A," "Burn Shop B," and Aliang's shop is burned down. Do you know who Aliang is?

SUDIN I already told you, it wasn't me who burned down Aliang's shop. Not me! The police already took my sworn statement, in quadruplicate. Four sheets of my testimony, Marwan! Hold on, are you really planning on getting away with what you just said? You clearly said we were stupid. All you have to do is answer: yes or no!

MARWAN Son of a bitch. Not "we" Sudin, "you". You're the stupid one. I've never believed that crap because I'm not stupid.

SUDIN Traitor!

MARWAN I never agreed to any violent action, from the start. So don't blame me if I tell everyone in town that tomorrow morning you're planning on stirring up trouble on the roads.

SUDIN Traitor! You'd better watch out. I'm going to tell the leader. You will face the consequences.

Sudin angrily exits through the shop entrance. Marwan follows after him.

MARWAN Sudin! Hey, Sudin!! *(re-entering the shop and to Selma)* Please excuse the commotion. We often have these kinds of loud disagreements, but they're over quickly. So how are you holding up? Rooting for Portugal or North Korea? *(laughs)* Please send my regards to Mr. Tom.

Marwan rushes out of the shop.

SIMPO It's all becoming clear now. That statue is indeed the source that started the ruckus in town. If they are really planning something... Can we remain silent? Imagine, try to imagine this scenario. A fengshui field spreads evenly throughout the town, thanks to the Earth Deity Temple. Then suddenly, a dragon statue, the Naga Statue, fraudulently sucks up all the powerful good fortune and directs it to a single point, namely Mr. Tom's inn. It's no wonder that mob is angry, because we have the right to be angry. Don't we? Let's get to the bottom of this situation by questioning Mr. Tom's true motives. We've been fooled since the protests began a year ago. We believed the Naga Statue was a symbol of pride for our town since its residents are predominantly ethnic Chinese. Mr. Tom is the instigator of the unrest and deserves to be blacklisted! And that statue needs to be demolished!

LINGLING   Where's my husband-to-be? How come he's not here yet?

SIMPO *(yelling at Selma)* If there's anyone who deserves to he hated in this town, it's your husband. Mr. Tom is the one to blame. Do you hear me?

SELMA   I have nothing to do with this business.

LINGLING *(to Mr. Goen)* Okay, it all makes sense now. It's already past 7 o'clock. Mr. Goen, why don't you answer me? My future Taiwanese husband said he'd arrive at 5:00. It's obvious now that you are planning someone else for my future husband. Just admit it, Mr. Goen, admit it. Why have I spent all this time taking such good care of my teeth? Because I believed what you said about Taiwanese men being fussy about teeth. My future is cursed. Thirty-two times I trained with you. I even promised to continue servicing you even though you're married. Do you not believe me? Look at my breasts, look…

SIMPO *(to Selma)* You must have known all about this. Isn't that right? You can't dodge my questions anymore by saying it's none of your business. I'm going to give you a bit of advice if what Sudin says really does take place tomorrow. You should run away. Now. I can no longer guarantee this shop will be safe.

SELMA   I'm not listening to you, Simpo! *(offended, she stands)* My apologies, gentlemen. This shop must close now. I please ask that you total up your food and drink tabs. I then ask that you please continue your discussions in another shop.

MR. GOEN *(to Selma)* For heaven's sake. Don't get taken in by two-bit provocations coming from Simpo's ignorant mind. After all, your husband is a hero in this town. Isn't that right, Simpo? There are circumstances when even a hero can make a mistake. It's normal. Like in my case as well. Sometimes even the best-laid plans for a good cause can fall short of expectations. I am always doing what is best for this town. But then, for example, the Taiwanese man wasn't able to make it today. It's clearly only a small piece of a much larger struggle.

An elegant man enters the shop. Simpo and Mr. Goen stand and greet him happily.

MR. GOEN Aaaaah Mr. Tom! This is no coincidence! We were just talking about how gracefully and heroically the Naga Statue stands in the intersection. I was just saying to Simpo how the proportions of the statue complement the vitality of the Earth Deity Temple built by our ancestors over one hundred years ago. Isn't that right, Simpo?

SIMPO Yes. What Mr. Goen says is correct. Exactly.

MR. GOEN I've been asking since midday why my right hand keeps twitching and why the sky overhead has become so bright. Apparently this is the reason why. It's that I was to see the vitality of Mr. Tom's resplendent face. But unfortunately, it seems we must say goodbye. There's a small errand I need to take care of, so please forgive me for breaking up this happy meeting. Come on Simpo, let's say goodbye. Lingling, give Mr. Tom's hand a kiss so his blessings increase your good fortunes. Ah, it's too bad we are in such a hurry. Wishing you continued success Mr. Tom! Thank you ma'am, your shop is such a comfortable place to stay and chat.

Tom watches with surprise as the three customers hurriedly exit. Lingling appears to want to remain, but Mr. Goen forcefully drags her out.

Selma quickly clears and cleans the tables. She fixes her hair.

SELMA Rika, Nina, close the shop now. Turn on the TV, and then you may go home. *(To Tom)* The match begins in fifteen minutes.

TOM What was up with those people? They hurried out of here the moment I arrived. What were they saying about me?

SELMA So what? Don't be so touchy. This is a coffee shop. People have the right to come and go as they please. Why do you have to feel offended? The match is in fifteen minutes. I need to connect your internet first. So keep quiet and don't bother me. *(She takes out a laptop from the table under the cash register and* *turns it on.)* So are you still rooting for Portugal over North Korea 2 to 1? I'll play your numbers but don't blame me if you're less lucky tonight.

TOM   What do you mean by "less lucky"?

SELMA   I'm not in a good mood, Tommy. I don't like being forced to close my shop to comply with your wishes.

TOM   Hey, haven't we already discussed this? Come on, don't start something that's going to make me have to raise my voice. What were they talking about? It's definitely not something to do with the shop that has put you in a bad mood. Definitely not.

SELMA   I've already told you time and time again that I don't like it when my shop loses out to soccer. You've always known I don't like soccer, yet you've forced me to learn all about it, and I gave in to your wishes. Plus, we had an agreement that my shop's affairs are non-negotiable. What's the difference between betting on soccer at home and betting on soccer in the shop? Isn't it more comfortable at home? I've been forced to give into your wishes, again. But in all other business affairs, you take sole charge.

TOM   So my hunch was right. They were talking about me. Those rascals didn't actually have to leave the moment I arrived. Come on, tell me. What were they talking about, Selma?

SELMA   Why don't you just ask them yourself?

TOM   Women! Why not make the tiniest effort to understand the simplest of things? Your shop is non-negotiable and it's your business. But my fengshui is also non-negotiable, and we agreed on that.

SELMA   Okay, okay, okay. We're done talking about it. For luck, the place you must watch is in the shop, because the shop has a cash flow aura. Because the negative air discharged by too many people will affect the score, only a maximum of two people can watch, namely you and me, and I'm required because, as the female shop owner, I radiate positivity. If your clothes bring good luck the first time you wear them, then the same clothes must always be worn so that the aura of good fortune attached to them is not lost. The direction of the television must be facing straight and right in the middle. The chair you sit in to watch may not be moved from where it is initially placed. That's the one-sided agreement I heard, is there something I'm still missing? Oh yeah, that I have to enter the score numbers on the internet because you don't care much for technology and so you can't do it yourself. For crying out loud Tom, what's the point of seeking knowledge if, in the end, all you believe in is superstition? I am truly baffled by this utter nonsense.

TOM Enough! I said enough. Don't wreck your good energy tonight with an unnecessary quarrel. For the last time, we're done talking about it. Full stop. Okay? How many more minutes until the match begins? Are you connected to the internet yet? That's your only job right now.

Rika and Nani finish closing up the shop. The two stand up to announce their departure.

RIKA Everything is in order, ma'am. My apologies, but starting tomorrow I won't be working here anymore. I'll soon be married to a Taiwanese man, and beginning tomorrow morning I'll be prepping at Mr. Goen's house. This is my own decision, I swear. Please forgive me for any shortcomings while I worked here.

SELMA Oh my God! Didn't I repeatedly warn you that the thousands of Chinese girls from this town who marry Taiwanese men end up as victims, suffering and broken? Only a few dozen have ever returned in a good place, but most of them, hundreds of them, return destitute, humiliated and disabled. Hundreds of others go missing, with their families never hearing any news about them ever again. So you have been truly poisoned by this scumbag's nonsense. Rika? My God!

RIKA Please forgive me. Mr. Goen warned me that you would say that. That you would tell me a bunch of lies to get me to keep working for you for criminally low wages like most people around here. My apologies, please forgive me. I have already made my decision.

SELMA Good heavens, Rika, Rika, how old are you, Rika? It's a shame that your judgement isn't yet mature enough to grasp how your life's going to end up. Yeah, whatever, it's up to you. Go on, go home and then meet that damn swindler. My God! For love of the God of Heaven, for the gentle and loving Goddess Kwan Im, forgive me. Oh God! And you, Nani, are you also quitting?

NANI No, ma'am, I'm not quitting yet. Mr. Goen is satisfied for now with Rika. It will be my turn next month.

SELMA God of Earth, God of the Universe. Forgive them. Now leave, both of you leave. Go on!

Rika and Nani hurriedly exit the shop. Tom smirks. Selma, with a sad face, is stunned. Lights slowly fade. Blackout.

Lights back up. The television broadcasts the World Cup match between Portugal and North Korea. Loud trumpeting and cheering is heard on the TV.

TOM How many more matches until the World Cup is over? Looks like Argentina is going to win. Hey, did you hear me? Never mind. Don't bother with insignificant things like that. Your real task has begun. We agreed.

SELMA Yeah, I've been listening. I'm backing Germany and Brazil, not Argentina.

TOM Remember the 2002 World Cup? Ronny smashed his TV set because Germany lost.

SELMA That was a different year, not now. I really can't get over how gamblers behave. What are they looking for? Like that Ronny. Rich, has a beautiful wife, sleeps and eats well every day. What's lacking that he feels the need to destroy his television and be unhappy? How much money does he make from all that unhappiness?

TOM Don't ever say bad things about Ronny to my face, okay? Listen, Ronny and I were a couple of crazy fools when we were young. He'd often throw the mic and slap the girls' butts in the karaoke room, and he'd happily pay the costs afterwards. So how much is he out if he chucks a single television set? *(laughs)* Ronny, Ronny, once, while he was shitfaced, he drew his friend's pistol and "Bang!" Those of us in the room were completely shocked and panicked. Ronny was detained. And you know what? He was only held two times twenty-four hours. It was his security guard friend, the pistol owner, who got the book thrown at him.

He was sentenced to twenty-four months and fired from his job. Ronny, Ronny...

SELMA It's that type of idiotic life I will never understand. It's the same with you. Drunk every night. And proud to tell the story of your pal who reached for a bottle of mineral water that he mistook for the car gear shift. What's so damn funny about that?

TOM That particular friend of mine really knows how to drink. Ah, forget it... Any type of alcohol is like water to him. Oh yeah, did I ever tell you, Ronny almost divorced his wife because she suddenly became pregnant?

SELMA Really, just why do I need to know this story?

TOM Ronny knew that his wife was using an IUD for birth control. But she suddenly got pregnant. They had a huge fight. Ronny couldn't understand and demanded his wife tell him who got her knocked up. In the end, they split up until their baby was born. After the DNA test, wild man Ronny suddenly began talking about God's miracles. Ronny left the entertainment business. He said their youngest child was a gift from God to make him realize that without human greatness, we can't combat... *(yells at the television set)* Damn! Goal. The defense sucks. They need to stick close to the offense! *(To Selma)* And you! How many times have I told you, I've bet money on this. Help me be observant. If the ball is in play against a dangerous opponent, tell me! You're too focused on getting me to talk about this and that. Breaking my concentration. God damn it!

SELMA Hey, what's up with that, Tommy? Why am I to blame? As if anyone's encouraging your mindless blathering. Besides, how could I control who scores a goals or not from this far away? This is totally messed up.

TOM Enough! Now shut it. Can't you shut the fuck up? *(A moment of silence.)* Years of living with me and she still doesn't understand me. How could you not know my personality and the way I do things?

SELMA What are you saying Tommy? So you think you know me? Know what colour clothing I like to wear? Know which foods I like to eat and the ones I avoid? Is it when I try to remind you that it's our 14th anniversary, but you prattle on and on about the Brazil-Chile match instead.

TOM When in the past have you ever dared talk to me like this? Now, suddenly you grow a pair. Feeling unstoppable, huh. I purchased you at a very high price; it was your family that made the sale to my father. So there was no need to speak romantically and whisper sweet nothings. It was much more important to focus on how to live a prosperous life than celebrate a wedding anniversary. If you don't like me, please, choose some other man out there. You just turned 30. You're pretty enough. Your body is still fresh and slim. Surely, there are plenty who'd line up for you.

SELMA So this is the direction our discussion is going? You are totally outrageous.

TOM How so? It's protracted rage. Let's end it tonight. I don't want us to have any obstacles in either of our hearts. You can express anything you want. Tonight, I'll listen to you.

SELMA Fine. I'll speak now, and we'll finish now. How many times have you said the word "now"? Hundreds of times. Enough already, I'm tired. For years, I've partnered with and served a drunkard. No need to say how cleaning your vomit off the bed made me sick to my stomach. No need to recount how many times I fulfilled every one of your requests from morning till dawn the next day. I haven't had a restful sleep in years!

Look, really take a look. I have to stay awake until dawn just to keep you company as you watch soccer. I've said a thousand times how much I detest soccer. But you say I must, and so I do. Why? I only do it to be accommodating. And what's funny, when you lose a bet based on those bullshit superstitious rules you've devised for the stupid ball games, it's me you blame.

TOM Hey, watch what you're saying. I've never made you do anything. Scram. Go to sleep. You're finished, right?

SELMA Finished? Hah, easy for you to say finished. Do you remember how many thousands of times you've said "finished"?

TOM Quit being so cryptic. Just tell me clearly what you want! We can forget about the next match coming up on TV.

SELMA It's not worth it to keep talking. You'll just go berserk for days, and there's no way out for me other than feeling sorry for myself. I really don't know why I keep this up. Maybe I've gone insane.

TOM Have you fallen for some other guy? Yeah, probably. I get it. I'm a drunk, gamble from time to time, and I like all the fun. But I'm not like those other jealous wimps. If you leave me, I'll smile and throw a huge party for my wife.

SELMA Oh, that's truly beautiful. What an expansive heart you have. Alright, I salute you. So now I'll keep it simple. What I want right now is a deep, restful sleep. I miss the coziness, like my dreams when I first agreed to marry you. But never mind, it's no good for us to raise a stink like this in the middle of the night. I surrender, Tom. Don't I always give up?

They both fall silent. Their eyes glaze over. The sounds of trumpets and cheers from the television grow louder.

Lights fade to black momentarily then rise slowly just enough to make out Tom and Selma in silhouette. They are so close to each other that it looks like they could be hugging.

TOM So I'm the reason you don't sleep well?

SELMA My love, you think that's the most important question?

TOM I don't intend to always put the blame on you. It's just that you aren't intelligent enough to understand my way of talking. If I clearly blame you for something, then it really is your fault.

SELMA *(giggling)* What did you say?

TOM Hey, why did you wash my red shirt yesterday without my permission?

SELMA You'd already worn that shirt for a week, my love. You couldn't smell its toxicity?

TOM My love, you've forgotten my smell. Only I wear that shirt. I'm not bothered by any smell. That is one of my good luck shirts.

SELMA *(giggling)* We can't control the outcome of the match, my love. Even if you're wearing your lucky shirt. Winning and losing is part of everyone's lot in life. If you dare to join the fray, you must expand your spirit when you lose.

TOM I'm always expanding my spirit. But you are always looking for trouble. You moved my chair, remember? Despite the fact I reminded you it was in my lucky position. The proof is that I lost that time you moved it.

SELMA Alright, in the future I won't disturb anything that belongs to you. You're ridiculous. But I ask you to understand this. Once in a while think about my feelings. Remember the time a gecko crawled on me out of the blue and I was totally taken by surprise? You shushed me and demanded I not move. You knew how scared I was at the time. You were on the side of the gecko because its tail was split in two. You said that because it was a rare gecko, it was bringing good luck and mercy. And I had to hold still until that gecko crawled off me. Do you find that funny?

TOM *(chortles)* Oh yeah, I remember. But it proved to be true, right? That kind of gecko brings great luck. Such gecko tails are sought after and sold at high prices by those who understand those sorts of things. You're just an ignoramus.

SELMA Look, you're going to lose tonight. *(laughs)* There will be no 2 to 1 score, it will end with a big fat zero. Believe me, I understand more about the game than you because I've learned all the tricks the top players use. That's the result of you forcing me to learn about soccer plays. Tommmm, my husband, ah, my love, my love, my love…

Lights fade slowly to a momentary blackout. Lights up slowly to full. Tom sleeps in a chair. Women's clothes are scattered across the floor.

From afar, sounds of an approaching convoy of motorcycles and cars on the street in front of the shop. Noises include revving engines and the mob yelling: "Tear down the Naga Statue! Destroy the Naga Statue!" "Burn Selma's shop!"

Lights out.

The End.

Hanna Fransisca

Hanna Fransisca, an award winning poet and fiction writer, is one of the few Chinese-Indonesian women writing plays. Hanna was born in Singkawang, West Kalimantan, an Indonesian province on the island of Borneo. Her work has been published in several leading newspapers, journals, and magazines including *Kompas Daily, Suara Merdeka, Koran Tempo, Malang Pos, Pikiran Rakyat, Horizon,* and *Sajak Journa*l. Overall, her works focus on Chinese-Indonesian culture based on her experiences growing up in Singkawang and the ethnic conflicts she observed resulting from discriminatory policies targeting Chinese communities during the New Order regime (1966-1998). The themes she tackles are particular to her personal trials as a member of a marginalized minority culture in Indonesia and at the same time speak to all women struggling to maintain their selfhood in the face of patriarchy.

Her first short story *Darahku Tumpah di Kelenteng* was an official selection of the 2008 Jakarta International Literary Festival. Two years later she published her first book of poetry *Konde Penyair Han* that won the *Tempo* Award for Best Poetry Book of 2010 and was shortlisted the same year for the Khatulistiwa Literary Award. The following year, Hanna was named *Tempo* Magazine's Outstanding Writer of the year. Her first collection of short stories, *Kolecer dan Hari Raya Hantu* was published in 2012, followed that same year by another short story collection *Sulaiman Pergi ke Tanjung Cina*, a novel *Kayu Kayu Dewa Dapur* and her first play, *Kawan Tidur (Bedfellows)*. In 2015, a second book of poetry, *A Man Bathing and Other Poems* was published by the Lontar Foundation in a trilingual edition featuring her original Indonesian poems translated into English and German.

Hanna claims that she wrote *Kawan Tidur (Bedfellows)* because Gunawan Maryanto, one of the founders of the Indonesian Dramatic Reading Festival (IDRF), challenged her to write a play (he was on the prowl for plays to include in the 2010 IDRF). *Kawan Tidur* was first read during IDRF in 2010 and 2011, then performed by Teater Tetas. In September 2018, *Kawan Tidur* was read at the Jejak-Tabi Exchange Festival in Kuala Lumpur, Malaysia. In May 2019 *Bedfellows* was given a staged reading at The Ovalhouse Theatre in London in the English translation by Cobina Gillitt.

Cobina Gillitt

Cobina is a freelance new play and production dramaturg, translator of Indonesian plays, and a member of Putu Wijaya's Teater Mandiri based in Jakarta. For over thirty years, she has performed and organized workshops with this leading theatre group in Indonesia and internationally, as well as serving as its company manager. She is an active member of the PEN America Translation Committee and the

Literary Managers and Dramaturgs of the Americas (LMDA). Since 2014, she has been a member of the faculty in the Conservatory of Theatre Arts, at Purchase College, State University of New York, where she teaches courses on Asian theatre, play adaptation, performance theory, theatre history, and dramaturgy for the Theatre and Performance major.

Some of Cobina's other translations of Indonesian plays include *OH* by Putu Wijaya in *100 DRAPEN* (Pentas Grafika, 2018) as well as *Ought* by Putu Wijaya, *Noah's Ark II* by Aspar Paturusi, and *Make Note!* by Rita Matu Mona and more that can be found in two anthologies she edited and for which she wrote the introductions: *The Islands of Imagination I: Modern Indonesian Plays* (University of Hawaii Press, 2014) and *The Lontar Anthology of Indonesian Drama, Volume 3: New Directions, 1965–1998* (University of Hawaii Press, 2017/Lontar Foundation, 2010). Examples of her scholarly publications include "A Legacy of Theatricality: Antonin Artaud's Encounter with Balinese Gamelan" in *Performing Indonesia* (Smithsonian Institution, 2016) and "How the Fish Swims in Dirty Water: *Antigone* in Indonesia" in *Antigone on The Contemporary World Stage* eds. Erin Mee and Helen Foley. (Oxford University Press, 2011)

Playwright's Note:

Since 2015 Kala Teater has initiated and worked on the *City in Theatre Project*. The *City in Theatre Project* is a reading project focusing on city issues through research with city residents. In 2015, three main issues were discussed in the city of Makassar, namely traffic jams, waste management and billboards, and the annual floods.

The *City in Theatre Project* in 2017 and 2018 involved input from 327 respondents who were residents of Makassar City. The study was conducted to understand their perceptions and views on the three issues faced by the city of Makassar, namely the reclamation of Losari Beach, the rise in the number of those with mental illness, and the act of suicide. The study was conducted through questionnaires and interviews with citizens of the city of Makassar.

The three issues were then explored in three performances called Gi*ve Me the Old Beach*, *The Madness of the Mad*, and *Don't Die Before He Arrives*. In addition, there was also a collaboration with four poets: Alfian Dippahatang, Faisal Oddang, Ibe Palogai, and Mariati Atkah. Their poems about the city of Makassar were incorporated into the performances.

The three performances of the *City in Theatre Project* used the creation strategy of documentary theatre, which Jean-Paul Sartre called the *theatre of fact*. Research materials consisted of interviews, questionnaires, newspaper articles, videos, audio recordings, which were given an aesthetic treatment for the stage. Scenes were created from a montage of events taking place simultaneously. Texts were composed from a juxtaposition of research, poetry and the dramatic text.

The show takes place in three different rooms. The audience moves from one room to the next. The audience should have a bodily experience that departs from the habitual. The audience is positioned as an active one which has the freedom to determine its own positions, movements and responses when engaging with the performance.

The three performances in the *City in Theatre Project* are presentations on the reality of life in the city of Makassar. The three performances are expected to be able to reflect the citizens' contribution in shaping the identity of the city of Makassar.

THE MAKASSAR TRILOGY

Shinta Febriany

Characters

Although Actors A, B, C and D are referred to in the text with male pronouns, they can be played by actors of any gender.

FIRST PRESENTATION
DON'T DIE BEFORE HE ARRIVES

A narrow space that resembles a long corridor with walls on the left and right. A space that oppresses the actors and the audience. A kind of elongated proscenium. The audience is only on one side, at a distance of only 1 metre from the performance space. Ropes hang from above. Ropes that wish to kill a person. Or many people.

SCENE 1
THE RED LIGHT OF DEATH

A red light glares at the audience for 40 seconds. The warm light of death. Actor A enters the space, standing with his back to the red light. His head is wrapped in a red plastic bag. He tries to suppress the voices in his head, making it difficult to breathe. His body is black from sadness. He looks at the people in front of him. It is like looking at a future death.

Actors B, C and D enter the space. They stand with their backs to the red light. Their heads are wrapped in red plastic bags. They look at the people in front of them, trying to communicate hidden feelings from their minds and bodies, minds and bodies whose only wish is to cease to exist. To die.

SCENE 2
LOVE IS DANGER

The sound of rain. Or wind. Love exists inside the actor's body. A dangerous love. It pushes the actor's body into a narrow space of the mind, into a death that has been planned. Actor A's body jerks forward, and then he walks slowly towards the audience, jerks again, walks slowly again. Actor B follows with the same actions. Actor C and Actor D perform the same actions in place. Actor A stands 1 metre away from the audience. His head drops. Actor B stands in the centre of the right side of the space. The sound of rain or wind disappears.

Poetry about the bitterness of love comes from behind. From the darkness of the mind. Love is a danger that can manifest itself in the decision to commit suicide. Why did love put danger into his body? Actor C recites a poem.

ACTOR C You were silent when I asked you
do you love me in return?
You refused to talk when I asked you
to show me what I had to do
so you would share your life with me.[1]

SCENE 3
PAKARENA[2] IN HIS BODY

Actor A begins to spin, putting the Pakarena into his body. Where is culture when suicide crosses your mind? Where does the government stand? Actor A utters poetry while letting the Pakarena continue to manifest itself in his body. Over time his body shrinks like a body without hope, a body which wants to disappear.

ACTOR A We have a government that has many mouths.
They always need a lot of words
that they eventually seize from us.[3]

Actor C and Actor D walk, leaving behind a government which likes to talk about global cities while economic factors continue to be the main drivers of suicide. The hands of Actor C and Actor D extend to call those who are already dead. Without any voice. Their words have been consumed by poverty and suffering.

SCENE 4
A LIST OF SUICIDES

Actor B utters a list of suicides. His voice sounds like a radio or television announcer. He walks from one rope to another. The ropes become microphones. The tragedies are announced so that they will not happen again. He swings the ropes back and forth. The tragedy of suicide lives in the past, but it may also live in the future.

ACTOR B   Doctor Yansos Djaya Sitorus, 50, was found dead by hanging on 27 December, 2018. Police Brigadier Arifin, 40, died after shooting his head with his own weapon on 4 April, 2017.

Hidayatullah was found dead by hanging on 27 July, 2017, after making a video call to his girlfriend.

Lebu Daeng Gassing, 55, was found dead by hanging on 12 January, 2018, using his grandson's swing rope.

Muhammad Rijal, 17, was found dead by hanging on 28 March, 2018. The victim had a mental illness.

Abdul Karim K, 38 years old, died hanging himself on 14 April, 2018. Before carrying out the deed the victim had looked agitated and was shouting.

Rostina Daeng Ti'no, 38 years old, died after drinking insecticide on 4 June, 2018. Darmawan, 26, died after slitting his own throat on 6 August, 2018. The victim could not tolerate the whispering voices in his head.

Actor A listens to the list of suicides and stamps his feet, jumps up and down, makes the sound of rustling plastic bags in front of Actor A's face, hugs Actor C and Actor D, and covers his face with his shirt. As if sadness was scattered throughout his body.

Actor C and Actor D also listen. Every now and then they turn to Actor B. Actor D stops. His body begins to sway, as if he is trying to recover the list of suicides from his memory. His hands press against his ears, not wanting to hear the sound of his own pain.

ACTOR D   Yoshua Flint Figerald, 19 years old, on 20 August, 2018 was found dead after hanging himself using a dog chain.

Nawaria, 80 years old, on 17 May, 2018, was found dead after hanging herself with a nylon rope.

Asma Yakub, 22 years old, on April 24, 2018, was found dead hanging under her house after returning from a Community Service Programme.

Kuni, 31 years old, on 22 April, 2018 died after recklessly plunging into the Bakaru hydropower dam.

Sk, 18 years old, on 10 April, 2018, was determined to swallow mosquito repellent because of a breakup with a boyfriend.

Norma, 21 years old, on 20 March, 2018, committed suicide by drinking herbicide after nightmares and spirit possession.

Dedy, 26 years old, died by hanging on 29 July, 2017. The victim suffered from a mental illness.

Actor C beats his chest while walking backwards. Suicide is a backwards journey. On that journey one carries a big hole in the chest. A big hole that is void of faith. Actor A makes the sound of death from his mouth. Actor B hugs the wall, rubs his body against the silent wall. Death is silent. Suicide is an attempt to be silent.

SCENE 5
THE DARKNESS OF DESIRE

The image of death manifests itself as an exit door for problems that cannot be solved by one's self and the conditions of reality. Have suicidal thoughts ever visited your head? Actor A and Actor C secrete the data drawn from the darkness of their desires while producing small movements from their bodies. Movements echoing one another.

While the data is being leaked, Actor B jogs backwards while striking his forehead, then jogs forward while striking the back of his head. Actor D also runs back and forth while striking his face. The data is hurting their minds and bodies. They are part of the data. Maybe the data is us as well.

ACTOR A A knife was the one thing I could see clearly.
ACTOR C Now only razor blades understand my feelings.
ACTOR A I swallowed six blister packs of my grandmother's medicine.
ACTOR C No diploma. No work.
ACTOR A In the name of love I'm willing to die for your happiness.
ACTOR C It's better to die than to suffer.
ACTOR A My life, my dreams, my future has been shattered.
ACTOR C Maybe this poison isn't as bitter as my life.
ACTOR A My family didn't accept me. Maybe God will accept me.
ACTOR C My jealousy towards you makes me want to sleep forever.
ACTOR A Our long fights made me tighten this rope around my neck.
ACTOR C The scraping of the knife bothered me less than those unseen voices.
ACTOR A That woman looks beautiful in your eyes. This shampoo tastes sweet in my throat.
ACTOR C The debt of my life will be paid off with the bang of a gun at my head.
ACTOR A I battle my disappointment by jumping from this building.
ACTOR C With this poison I will catch up with my husband.
ACTOR A Goodbye!

The actors stop moving right after "goodbye" is said by Actor A. The sound of sadness enters the space. The red light comes back, glaring at the audience. God has not arrived.

The actors walk hurriedly. Randomly. Colliding. They fall then get up and walk again. The ropes also move, swinging with the inevitability of death. God has not arrived.

At one point the actors' bodies start to tremble. Maybe for 120 seconds. Then they walk out of the first space to the second space.

SECOND PRESENTATION
THE MADNESS OF THE MAD

A space which is similar to the space used for the first presentation: long and restricted. A space that makes it possible for the performance and the audience to be in an intimate environment. The audience is at a distance of only 1 metre from the performance space. Clothes are strewn on the floor, suggesting a life of destitution.

SCENE 1
PUTTING ON IDENTITIES

The sound of a Makassar drum. A man stands behind the audience while playing the drum. Two minutes later the actors enter the space. The man walks into the space while still playing the drum. The actors start to perform their "madness".

Actor A walks around while occasionally threatening the audience and the other actors. Actor B walks around with his legs wide with the swagger of a rap artist. Actor C considers himself an artist. He seduces the audience, blowing kisses. Actor D watches the audience and other actors. The atmosphere is chaotic. Occasionally the actors collide and start to threaten each other. Sometimes they chase one another, jump, laugh and play with one another.

They shout the names and ages of people with mental illness while putting on the clothes scattered on the floor. As if they are putting on various identities onto their bodies. Identities which they do not recognize. They repeat the list of people while continuing to put clothes on their bodies. Their bodies grow large, with the mass of other lives. Now, their bodies are crammed with various identities from a barely understood past.

ACTOR A   Fatima, 35 years old.
Espana Iqbal, 60 years old.
Arfandu Putra.
Kipli.

ACTOR B   Bahar, 40 years old.
Udin, 46 years old.
Aco, 19 years old.
Muhammad Rijal, 17 years old.

ACTOR C   Acai, 40 years old.
Gondolo, 45 years old.
Iqbal, 60 years old.
Koreng, 48 years old.
Melati, 32 years old.
Iwan, 25 years old.

ACTOR D   Pance, 70 years old.
Gassing, 85 years old.
Mussing, 60 years old.
Baco Tola, 68 years old.
Minah, 72 years old.

SCENE 2
DELIRIUM FROM THE PAST

Actor C stands at the right side of the space, swinging his hands slowly and picking up speed until they are moving very fast. He gazes evenly at the audience. Actor A and Actor D sit side by side in the centre of the left side of the space. Actor A scratches his body.

Actor D has the illusion that he is smoking. Actor B walks slowly at the back.

Suddenly Actor D stands up and claps. His face is full of smiles. Actor A keeps on scratching. Actor B keep on walking. Actor D also starts to scratch his body. Actor C starts rambling about war and heroism, excerpts from a poem. Delirium from the past, haunting them, which none of them can understand. All the actors are delirious.

ACTOR C   There the statue of myself must stand after the guests have gone with a defeat that they cannot fathom.[4]

Actor C slides to the back. Back and forth. Actor A and Actor D simultaneously scratch themselves. Actor B becomes a hero. Actor D rushes to hug actor C, and starts rambling from another poem, about a lover who fails to return.

ACTOR D   I heard the sound of ships coming, but there was no you.[5]

Actor C hurls Actor D to the floor and slaps his cheeks as if to wake him up from his delirium. But madness has already seized him. Actor A flings himself backwards and forwards. His body continues to be in a state of delirium. Actor B hugs Actor D who has fallen. They dance and appear happy.

ACTOR B   This city, the last place we waved at each other, has changed beyond recognition.[6]

The sound of drums. All actors dance in unison. Their faces offer a variety of expressions, one after another, until they become fatigued, and collapse onto the floor. Their bodies pile over one another, surrendering to the unconscious.

SCENE 3
SOUNDS OF MADNESS

All the actors slowly rise and slap the floor with their palms. Soft sounds at first, and then rising to a chaotic crescendo. Madness is a sound within each body. Some sounds are loud while others are partly muted or emitted softly. The actors continue to produce the sounds of madness while jumping as high as possible, scattering to occupy the back of the performance space.

Actor D suddenly runs to the corner while covering his ears. He does not want to hear the soundscape of his madness. Actor B jumps on Actor D's back, pulls his hair, hits his arms and struggles with him. An invitation to return to madness. Actor A and Actor C appear as monkeys or other animals. Actor B lies on the floor and then leaves in disappointment. Actor D follows him, grasping for a love that is no longer capable of seeing itself. He stops in his tracks.

Actor A and Actor C cover their faces with their clothes. Actor B and Actor D also cover their faces. The sound of madness emerges from one paragraph of poetry. The sound of madness that comes from disappointment, the inability to accept the demands of life.

ACTOR A Love is not important in this city, you said,
you only need a car and a well-stocked mall,
even though the streets are getting narrower
and poverty is the only thing
that still believes in love.[7]

SCENE 4
CELEBRATING THE LOSS OF IDENTITY

After the poem, the celebrations begin. The actors shout cheerfully, undress themselves and throw their clothes into the air. One by one the clothes are removed. One by one their identities are thrown into the space after being held captive in selves that have lost sight of the world. Over and over they recite celebratory texts about lost identities. Celebratory texts that contain both anger and pain.

ACTOR D	Hello boss! Freedom!
ACTOR A	There was my son but he was taken by flood.
ACTOR B	You bastard!
ACTOR C	You dog!

The celebratory texts are uttered while the actors interact with the space. Their clothes are slapped against the body and against the floor repeatedly. The voices of the actors rise to the ceiling of the space, and bounce off the audience. A strange, cheerful feeling grows within each actor, within the silent walls of the space. Therapeutic poetry is heard.

ACTOR B   Then I spread myself like silk.
I weave myself from threads of healing.[8]

ACTOR C   But there is no self in me
in my origins
and the fate line on my palm.[9]

SCENE 5
SEARCHING FOR ILLUSIONS

Actor A sings his resignation to the audience. It is a dangdut[10] song that wants to die many times. A madness that wants to make a home for itself.

ACTOR A
Kill me with your sword
as long as you don't kill me with your love.
I would rather die at your hands
than die at my own.[11]

Actor B, Actor C and Actor D start moving into the space of the audience, looking for reflections of themselves in the audience. The audience members seem to project images from the past into the minds of the actors. Various people who the actors believe to be their friend, husband, mother. Illusions everywhere. But the audience is reality.

ACTOR C	Girl, got a lipstick?
ACTOR B	Are you my husband?
ACTOR D	Darling, do you have a cigarette?
ACTOR A	Mum, give me some money!

SCENE 6
RELEASING IDENTITIES

Actor A is still humming. The actors walk away from the audience towards the furthest part of the space. They start to sway. The sound of drums. The actors turn their backs to the audience. Their bodies sway slightly as they sit down. The remaining clothes on their bodies are removed and then thrown onto the floor. Lights out. The sound fades.

Now, there is no identity in the self anymore.

THIRD PRESENTATION
GIVE ME THE OLD BEACH

A closed room. A white screen for moving images. The stage is empty.

SCENE 1
LOOKING AT THE SUNSET

An image of the sun about to set. The sound of waves fading. The audience watches the sun set for about 7 minutes. Then the screen goes dark. Silence spreads and touches the consciousness of the audience.

SCENE 2
LOSARI, RUNNING

Images of the current condition of the Losari Beach appear, in quick succession, like the reclamation work itself. Speed is a stealthy menace that will eventually destroy the city.

SCENE 3
SOUNDS OF LOSARI

An image of an actor sitting and looking at the sunset. Sadness fills the air. Voices from interviews can be heard. The din of city residents' opinions fills the space. Images of actors posing under heavy machinery, actors lying in the sand, and the reclamation of Losari Beach.

VOICES

1. In my opinion, the reclamation of Losari Beach in Makassar isn't done for the common people. It seems like it's intended only for people who have money and it actually sacrifices many social aspects of the lives of Makassar residents, especially those who live around the Mariso coast. After all, what's so important about reclamation when Makassar still has lots of land that's actually very suitable for housing? This reclamation only makes Makassar look better on the surface but basically it makes Makassar more fragile, destroying the livelihoods of many fishermen on the Mariso coast, affecting the social life of the residents there and creating other social crises that impact the community.

2. In my opinion, the reclamation of Losari Beach is like forcefully seizing the right of Makassar residents to be able to enjoy the beautiful sunset as they once used to do. In the past, when we wanted to see the sunset, the boundary between the sky and the sea was very clear, especially when the sun dipped into the sea and the sky immediately turned orange, and sometimes gold. If you try to see the sunset now it will be affected by the dunes from the reclamation. The reclamation of Losari Beach makes me miss the old sunset view. Now it's gone. Well, there's a view but there's additional stuff that's damaging a scenery that was once very beautiful, the most special one in the city of Makassar. Now the scenery has been spoiled by the very people we were supposed to trust.

3. About the reclamation of Losari Beach, actually I don't agree. Why? Because the reclamation will certainly have a lasting impact

on the environment, marine life, and ecosystems in the sea. That's just one aspect. It also means that new buildings will be constructed around the area. This will actually destroy our view of the sea or coast around Losari Beach so that aesthetically speaking this will no longer be a part of the beauty of Makassar. Another issue is that the reclamation has cut off the sources of income for the surrounding community. This community used to catch either clams or fish as a source of income for their families. That's just in terms of disruption of nature, of the environment, we haven't even touched on the legal aspects. Naturally the reclamation will have a legal impact. Why? Because there will be state lands that are legally and formally managed by the community, so they have management rights. And this must be considered carefully because sooner or later it might become a time-bomb where you have magnificent buildings standing on land whose management rights are owned by the community.

4. I can see the positive side to the reclamation on Losari Beach. For example, there are many macro industries that can be set up there, not only macro, but micro ones, like the vendors of grilled bananas and other foodstuff. But on the negative side, the beauty of Losari Beach can't be seen anymore now. And secondly, the pleasure of eating grilled bananas there is lost because there is no more sunset at Losari Beach. Also, the beach might be dirtier now. I've seen garbage on Losari Beach that's stinking up the beach and turning the water black. Those are some of my criticisms about Losari Beach. In essence, the sunset on Losari beach isn't as beautiful as it used to be.

SCENE 4
A PRESSING REALITY

The screen is dark for 10 seconds. The sound of the citizens' interviews has ceased. The actors cross from one end of the space to the other. One by one. The reality of reclamation is a pressing reality. The actors wish to leave that reality.

VOICES

5. In my opinion, regarding the development of the CPI (Central Point of Indonesia) project on Losari Beach, I disagree. Why? The main attraction for tourists who wanted to come to Losari Beach was the sunset but the reality is now they cannot see it anymore. The second thing is that it's no longer appropriate to call it 'Losari Beach' because there is no sand there. It's more appropriate to call the place a public square instead of Losari Beach.

6. So, in almost every city I've encountered coastal reclamation. This, as we already know, not only destroys dozens of marine life and aquatic habitats but most importantly, also destroys communities which for decades have depended on the sea for their livelihoods. What is interesting is that the reclamation often coincides with the construction of a magnificent mosque by the majority religious group, symbolising the grandeur of the city. Well, this has proven to be effective in persuading the community to fully support the development, including the reclamation process. The parties involved seem to deliberately carry out mystification in the name of religion to legitimise the damage they're doing. Reclamation just isn't good news.

7. In my opinion when it comes to beach reclamation, it's only natural that there are pros and cons. For the pros, it's to make Makassar more developed because one of the central gathering points in Makassar is Losari Beach. The reclamation was made to expand the Losari Beach area from 800 square meters to 5 square kilometres. For the cons, it's related to the environment because the sand material comes from the dredging of the coastlines of the Galesong and Takalar areas. And it actually does damage to the ecosystem there. The local residents are affected because of all the disruption. Sand dredging itself is detrimental to people around there. Just imagine the accumulation of sand that has been dredged and piled up along the coast. It surely requires a lot of sand material and it's quite damaging to the ecosystem there. That's in my opinion, as a layman. But overall, maybe we can just

trust that the Makassar City Government will know how to explain to local residents that their fears are unfounded. That it's indeed a real, pure, positive thing that they are building together with the goal of creating an advanced and global city of Makassar.

SCENE 5
POWER AND VOICES

An image of an actor running. The voices of the residents' interviews are heard again. Opinions flowing into the performance space. Images of machines doing their work.

VOICES

8. Not far from Losari Beach, there are about forty-five heads of families, who were driven out of the land where they have been farming, for the sake of smooth reclamation operations. Reclamation not only has a negative impact on the future of our environment, but has already wrecked the economic environment for coastal residents. We're now even beginning to lose the beauty of the sunset on Losari Beach and it's very sad.

9. Reclamation is a portrait of human greed displacing the habitats of fish and other marine life so as to create ivory towers, changing the face of the earth beyond God's authority. There might be beauty produced, but it's all artificial. Buildings gleam in the light but below them the street children sleep face down, shivering in the night wind.

10. As for my opinion about beach reclamation, we all know that Losari Beach is one of the most famous tourist attractions in South Sulawesi, Makassar, and even in Indonesia. When we mention Makassar, people will automatically think of the famous Losari Beach. The reclamation has made Losari Beach very different from what it used to be. And other than the impact on its beauty, there's a health impact where the rubbish or stagnant water between Losari Beach and the mounting piles of sand become more and

more dirty — a dumping ground and an eyesore. Furthermore, the reclamation has made it difficult to have a clear view of the sea. So, there's no longer a sense that there's a beach because of the coastal reclamation.

Actors run into the space and suddenly stop to look at the heavy equipment at work. The actors advance towards the machines as if they are preparing for a duel. Their hands create big shadows on the screen. But the heavy equipment is a force in its own right. The actors fall and are crushed several times, and finally leave the stage.

SCENE 6
RESISTANCE FALLS

Images of an actor falling from a concrete bench. Fast and repetitive. The sounds of the interviews become increasingly loud, with overlapping voices, filling the entire space. The resistance has fallen. The screen goes dark for 5 seconds.

SCENE 7
LOSARI IS THE MOON

Images of Actor C bringing a radio to a dock, turning it on, then leaving. The song, I Saw The Moon On Your Face by Sam Saimun, is heard. A song from the past that expresses loneliness. On Losari's face at this time the moon is not visible. Reclamation has covered part of her face.

SCENE 8
MOURNING RITUALS

Image of a sunset blocked by reclamation. The faint sound of waves. Actor C appears on stage carrying a microphone stand. The song I Saw The Moon On Your Face can be heard, faintly. Actor A, Actor B, and Actor D enter the stage with flowers covering their faces. They walk slowly down the stage, with sorrow in their laps. Actor C reads a mantra, a poem of despair.

ACTOR C   *The Body of the City[12]*

a single body falls to become a city, like the aorta, two rivers split through its heart, wondering where the direction to the estuary is, then twisting in the same strait. nipah trees call it Tallo, call it Jeneberang. one in the north the other in the south. collecting mud as Lakkang, a delta that is always being caressed by waves.

only sand and water foam understand why the arteries to Mangkasara are sailed by the boats known as the pinisi, palari and patorani. it was like that before. a long time ago. now it is only a memory that evaporates from under the epidermis layer. indeed, a body is a city which contains humans and their anxieties, and a past that is slowly disappearing. and a future that is rushing to arrive.

the things that bubble are the alveoli; villages that continue to run towards their suicides. pawning candlesticks for mercury lamps, finishing off the segmented fields, the swamps of Panakkukang, the shrubs of Mamajang. before the rushed farewells, perhaps there were a few things that could still be saved; the tall alang-alang grasses, a collection of ancestral histories, the old brick fortress at Ujung Pandang.

a body is a city. every one of its burrows contains a store of questions, holes for the various debris of life. people scattered like hair. then on Bontoala's chest, who knows who will be able to absorb the letters alif ba ta and understand the Quran. a mantra to revive the dead even though they have turned to fibres uprooted from the pores.

the body became feverish when it was abused by time, became angry when it was struck by a new world. a universe of objects. and all that scattered hair continued to be delirious over illusions. they're scattered from Mandai to Losari, only to find a tomb under the overpass. a tomb with a tombstone with their own names on it.

MAKASSAR, 2017

After the mantra is read, the Actor places a flower under the screen as if he is grieving for Losari and then leaves the stage. Actor C also places another flower and moves the microphone stand to the centre of the stage. He points the microphone at the audience, inviting them to speak. After staring at the audience for a while he leaves the stage.

The image of the sunset is slowly fading. The lights fade as well. The ritual is complete.

The End.

Glossary

1 – From the poem *Don't Fall in Love in This City* by Faisal Oddang.
2 – *Pakarena* is a traditional dance from South Sulawesi, accompanied by two-headed drums (*gandrang*) and a double reed oboe (*puik-puik*).
3 - From the poem *Don't Fall in Love in This City* by Faisal Oddang.
4 – From the poem *The Statue That Spoke* by Ibe S Palogai.
5 – From the poem *Requiem for the City* by Faisal Oddang.
6 – From the poem *Requiem for the City* by Faisal Oddang.
7 – From the poem *Don't Fall in Love in This City* by Faisal Oddang.
8 – From the poem *Welcome* by Ibe S Palogai.
9 – From the poem *Welcome* by Ibe S Palogai.
10 – *Dangdut* is a genre of Indonesian folk and popular music influenced by Hindustani and Arab styles.
11 – From the *dangdut* song *Resignation* that was popularized by Muchsin Alatas.
12 – A poem by Mariati Atkah.

Shinta Febriany

Shinta Febriany was born in South Sulawesi, Indonesia. She is the Artistic Director of Kala Teater, based in Makassar, South Sulawesi. In 2007, Shinta was awarded the Celebes Award from South Sulawesi Provincial Government for her dedication to theatre. Shinta graduated from the Theatre and Visual Art Studies programme at the Gadjah Mada University Graduate School. As a theatre director, playwright and poet Shinta's works are known for challenging gender stereotypes, exploring embodiment, and examining contemporary urban problems in East Indonesia.

Alfian Sa'at

Alfian is a Resident Playwright with W!LD RICE, one of Singapore's most recognised theatre companies. His published works include three collections of poetry, *One Fierce Hour*, *A History of Amnesia*, *The Invisible Manuscript*, a collection of short stories, *Corridor*, a collection of flash fiction, *Malay Sketches*, three collections of plays as well as the published play *Cooling Off Day*.

He has been nominated eleven times for Best Original Script at the Life! Theatre Awards, eventually winning in 2005 for *Landmarks*, in 2010 for *Nadirah,* published in *Southeast Asian Plays* (Aurora Metro, 2016), in 2013 for *Kakak Kau Punya Laki (Your Sister's Husband)* and in 2016 for *Hotel* (with Marcia Vanderstraaten).

In 2011, he was awarded the Boh-Cameronian Award in Malaysia for Best Book and Lyrics for the musical *The Secret Life of Nora*. In 2013, he won the Boh-Cameronian Award for Best Original Script for the play *Parah*.

In 2001, he won the Golden Point Award for Poetry as well as the National Arts Council Young Artist Award for Literature. He has also been nominated for the Singapore Literature Prize three times, for *Corridor* (Commendation Prize, 1999), *A History of Amnesia* (2004) and his translation of the novel *The Widower* (2016).

Playreading of *The Makassar Trilogy* IDRF 2018, Yogyakarta, directed by Ibed Surgana Yuga for Jaring Project. Photo: IDRF 2018 Documentation team *above*
Cut Off directed by Riyadhus Shalihin, performed in Selasar Sunaryo Art Space Bandung, 2016. Photo: Mega A Noviandari, *below*

The Silent Song of the Genjer Flowers, Institut Ungu Production at Goethe Haus, Jakarta, 2014. Directed by Faiza Mardzoeki. Photo: Adrian Mulya, *above*
Playreading of *Red Janger* directed by B. Verry Handayani at Asian Playwrights Meeting, Yogyakarta, 2019. Photo: Budi N.D. Dharmawan, *below*

Playreading at IDRF, Yogyakarta by Teater Tetas, 2010.
Photo: IDRF 2010 Documentation team, *above*
Playreading of *Sin* directed by Rosamunde Hutt at Ovalhouse Theatre, London, 2019. Photo: Steve Robson, *below*.